*The Genesis and Formation
of the World Council of Churches*

D1313350

The Genesis and Formation of the World Council of Churches

W. A. Visser 't Hooft

World Council of Churches, Geneva

280.1

ISBN No. 2-8254-0733-X
© 1982 World Council of Churches, 150 route de Ferney,
1211 Geneva 20, Switzerland
Printed in Switzerland

Contents

Preface

This book seeks to describe the process which led to the formation of the World Council of Churches in 1948. That process began with proposals made in Constantinople in 1919, and in Uppsala in the same year; it was completed with the attempt to define the nature of the World Council in 1950.

The book deals with the emergence of the idea of a world council, with the cold reception which first greeted it, with its temporary eclipse, its reappearance, its elaboration, the vote of confidence given to it by the churches in a time of crisis, its final acceptance by the first Assembly in 1948 and the attempt to define its nature at Toronto in 1950.

The book will also recall the pioneers, from different churches and various countries, who had the imagination and the tenacity to translate the ecumenical vision into concrete plans. They were able, through years of patient work, to convince a large number of churches that this was a necessary step forward towards the fulfilment of their common calling.

It is strange that no one has yet given a coherent and full account of this important development in modern church history. There are books and articles which tell part of the story. Some of these deal with the role played by particular churches,[1] while others describe the contribution of individual church leaders.[2] Others again concentrate on one particular stage in the development of the Council.[3] My own chapter, "The Genesis of the World Council of Churches", in the book, *A History of the Ecumenical Movement (1517-1948),*[4] does not deal adequately with the period in which the first proposals were made, and requires elaboration at many other points.

Of the many books by Roman Catholic writers dealing with the history of the ecumenical movement two are of special importance for our subject, namely the *Histoire doctrinale du mouvement œcuménique* of Gustave Thils[5] and *La signification ecclésiologique du Conseil œcuménique des Eglises* by Bruno Chenu.[6] Written in a truly ecumenical spirit and offering constructive critical judgment, they make a real contribution to the understanding of the ecumenical development. Although I disagree with some of their opinions, I have learned a good deal from them. But both books concentrate their attention on the period after World War II and deal therefore with the formation rather than with the genesis of the World Council.

Plans and proposals concerning a new world organization of the churches made before our century are outside the scope of this book. They are of interest in so far as they permit a comparison with the twentieth century project,[7] but they had no direct influence on those proposals and therefore do not belong to our story.

Plans of a more limited character, like those to unite the churches of one region, of one confession, or the Protestant churches alone, are also outside our scope. They form an important part of the total story of the ecumenical movement but they shed no light on the genesis of the World Council. Finally, international religious organizations which are based on individual membership or those which propose an inter-religious basis of cooperation have also no place in the genealogy of the World Council which seeks to bring together the churches on a specifically Christian basis and in a permanent fellowship.

Even among active participants in the life of the World Council there is an alarming ignorance about its origin and formation. Alarming not only because the achievements of our predecessors deserve to be better known, but also because we cannot understand the nature, the possibilities and the limitations of what we have inherited unless we know something about the way in which it was brought into being. Moreover, a number of questions concerning World Council policy which may seem quite new today arose already in earlier times, and we can learn a great deal from answers then given.

I do not belong to the generation of the men and women who took the daring initiative and proposed the creation of the World Council, but it has been my privilege to know most of these pioneers and to see them at work. From about 1933, I myself became involved in the process of formation. There are not many left today who lived through that time of ecumenical exploration and discovery. That is why I feel I must tell this story.

W. A. Visser 't Hooft

1. The proposal of the Church of Constantinople

When the Holy Synod of the Church of Constantinople — the Ecumenical Patriarchate — met on 10 January 1919, it took an initiative which was without precedent in church history. It was officially decided to take steps to issue an invitation to all Christian churches to form a "league of churches". Thus the Church of Constantinople became the first church to plan for a permanent organ of fellowship and cooperation between the churches. The meeting was presided over by the *locum tenens* of the Ecumenical See, Metropolitan Dorotheos of Brussa, who made the following statement:

> I think the time has already come for the Orthodox Church to consider seriously the matter of union of the different Christian churches, especially that with the Anglican, the Old Catholic and the Armenian churches. As the most significant announcement and recommendation for union of the different nations in a League of Nations have come from the great Republic of the United States of America in the Western world, so also the most significant announcement and recommendation for the study on the approach and the union of the different Christian denominations in a League of Churches ought to come from the Great Church of Constantinople in the East. Our Church therefore should take the initiative and after a thorough study on this subject give the impetus for the union of all churches in Christian love.[1]

This statement has several remarkable features. The proposed action was specifically ecclesiastical. It emanated from a church and was addressed to other churches. Its scope was wide, for it was proposed to include "all" churches in the League. The comparison with President Wilson's proposal concerning the setting up of a League of

Nations shows that Metropolitan Dorotheos was fully aware of the historical significance of his initiative.

The proposal was accepted by the Synod and a committee was appointed to prepare a report on the subject. The drafting was entrusted to the members of the faculty of the Theological School of Halki. The Dean of the Faculty, Germanos Strenopoulos, Metropolitan of Seleukia, is generally supposed to have written most of the text. He was a man of wide culture who, after receiving his degree at Halki, had studied at the Universities of Leipzig, Strasbourg and Lausanne. In 1911, at the Conference of the World Student Christian Federation in Constantinople, he had become acquainted with John R. Mott, Nathan Söderblom and other pioneers of the ecumenical movement. In April 1919, when a delegation of the American Episcopal Church visited Constantinople to inform the Patriarchate of the plan to hold a World Conference on Faith and Order, the Metropolitan of Cesaria was able to report on behalf of the synod that the special committee set up to study "the question of the league of the different churches and of their possible rapprochement" had already reached its conclusions.[2] The Holy Synod approved the Report of the Committee on 19 November and the Encyclical was sent out in January 1920.[3]

It has sometimes been suggested that the proposal from Constantinople for a League of Churches was inspired by Söderblom's plan for an Ecumenical Council, but this is most unlikely. In January 1919 when the Synod of the Patriarchate first discussed the question, Söderblom had not yet published the articles in which he formulated his ideas on the subject. It is true that his friend, the young Swedish diplomat Kolmodin, had been in contact with the Patriarchate since February 1918, and that he had certainly told of Söderblom's efforts to bring church leaders of different nations together, but there is no evidence to show that Söderblom made any reference in that year to an "Ecumenical Council". Söderblom himself spoke of the Constantinople plan as a proof "that the same thoughts influenced independently the hearts of Christians in different churches and nations".[4] What, then, did the members of the Holy Synod have in mind when they took their unusual initiative?

There was, in the first place, the grateful awareness of new opportunities to fulfill the calling of the Patriarchate. The collapse of the Ottoman Empire meant the end of an era in which the Church had not been able to carry out its mission in full freedom. In April 1919, the Metropolitan of Cesaria told the visiting delegation from the American Episcopal Church that the church has been surrounded for five centuries by unfavourable conditions and had been under constant and implacable persecution. Now the church "is exceedingly joyful that the desired opportunity has come for her to continue her former more general activity under more favourable conditions".[5] That general activity was first of all the strengthening of the fellowship of the churches in communion with Constantinople, but it included also the concern for fraternal relations with other churches. The ecumenical intention was clear from the fact that the Encyclical was addressed "Unto the Churches of Christ Everywhere" and that it affirmed that churches "should no more consider one another as strangers and foreigners, but as relatives, and as being a part of the household of Christ and fellow-heirs, members of the same body and partakers of the promise of God in Christ".[6] The synod felt that rapprochement and cooperation between the churches did not have to wait until doctrinal differences were overcome. The fraternal relations could prepare the way for the full unity of the church.

Archbishop Germanos himself said in 1929: "How wide the conception is which the Encyclical teaches at this point becomes clear in that it widens the notion of the relationships between the members of a single church — as members of one body according to St Paul's wonderful teaching — so as to apply it to the relationships between several churches".[7] It is clear from this that the proposed "League of Churches" was something more than a merely utilitarian arrangement, for it was described in biblical terms. To be sure, in the prevailing circumstances it could not be more than a stage in preparation for the full union which the churches had to seek, but it was possible nevertheless to use for this plan the word *koinonia*. That word can be used in an organizational sense, as in *koinonia* (League) of Nations, but the first sentence of the Encyclical shows that its authors used the word also in the spiritual sense.

In the second place, the Church of Constantinople believed that the proposal to form a League of Churches was timely because, for the first time in history, a League of Nations was being created. Twice in the Encyclical itself and again in the covering letter, the League of Nations was mentioned. The churches were warned: "How should they continue to fall piteously behind the political authorities who, truly applying the spirit of the gospel and of the teaching of Christ, have under happy auspices already set up the so-called League of Nations in order to defend justice and cultivate charity and agreement between the nations." It was therefore necessary to establish "a contact and league between the churches". The covering letter spoke of "the setting up of a league of churches *(Koinonia ton Ekklesion)* on the model of the League of Nations *(Koinonia ton Ethnon).*

For those who did not witness the appearance of the League of Nations on the international scene, this very strong emphasis on it as a wonderful new beginning will be surprising, for they know the story of its decline and the disappointment caused by its failure. But the Encyclical was written in the year 1919, the year in which the dream dreamt by so many philosophers, the dream of an international order based on law and justice, seemed at last to become a political reality.

The leader of the most powerful nation, President Woodrow Wilson, had made the proposal for the League of Nations the cornerstone of his policy at the Peace Conference. He had come to Europe at the end of 1918, and had met with a triumphal reception. On 25 January 1919 the Peace Conference decided to set up a special committee to draft the Charter of the League. This committee, of which President Wilson was the chairman, produced a report which was adopted by the Peace Conference on 29 April 1919, and the League of Nations came into being on 10 January 1920.

It was this League with its aura of purity which the Synod of Constantinople was using as a model, the League which had not yet been contaminated by the brutal world of political conflict. It is striking that the decision to suggest a League of Churches was made in the month in which the Peace Conference established its committee to work out a plan for a League of Nations, and further, that the Encyclical proposing a League of Churches was issued in the month in which the League of Nations was inaugurated. There had also been some personal contact between Constantinople and Paris, for the Metropolitan of Brussa, the *locum tenens* as Patriarch, visited the French capital in April 1919 to present the concerns of the Patriarchate. He had certainly been informed of the development of the plan for a League of Nations by the Greek statesman, Venizelos, who was a member of President Wilson's committee.

The Encyclical however indicated not only new opportunities, but also great dangers. It read: "... a sincere and close contact between the churches will be all the more useful and profitable for the whole body of the church, because many dangers threaten not only particular churches, but all of them. These dangers attack the very foundations of the Christian faith and the essence of Christian life and society." The general instability following World War I was felt all the more acutely by the Eastern churches, because the main elements of stability in their environment, the Russian and the Ottoman Empires, had suddenly collapsed. The relationship of the Patriarchate with the government of Tsarist Russia had not always been easy, but the Tsarist regime had consistently protected the interests of Orthodoxy. The Ottoman government had severely limited the freedom of the Patriarchate, but had allowed it to fulfill its main functions. The future was not a series of question marks. Would it bring about the realization of the "Great Idea", the repossession by the Greeks of Constantinople, the coming of a Greek *basileus* and the rededication of Hagia Sophia as the spiritual centre of Orthodoxy? Or would a more extreme Turkish nationalism gain power? In these uncertain circumstances, the isolation of the Patriarchate had to be overcome.

Another powerful reason to work for a cooperative relationship with other churches was the great harm done by the proselytizing activities of Western churches in the lands of the Eastern churches. The Encyclical continued: "So many troubles and sufferings are caused by other Christians and great hatred and enmity are aroused, with such insignificant results, by this tendency of some to proselytize and entice the followers of other Christian confessions." The Orthodox churches had been deeply hurt by the "sheep-stealing" in which a number of Western churches and missions were engaged. To treat Orthodox Christians as pagans who should be converted seemed to the Eastern churches as a denial of Christian solidarity. The proposed League should create such links between the churches that proselytism would become unthinkable.

The Encyclical did not enjoy a wide circulation. There was no address list of all the churches at that time. It was especially disappointing that churches which received the document did not react. Metropolitan Germanos recalled in 1948: "In the midst of their many problems, which had arisen after the war in each of the Christian churches, very little attention was given unfortunately (specially in the West) to the above Encyclical, and no answers of the churches eager to recognize the necessity of understanding and collaboration reached Constantinople."[8] In the summer of 1920, however, the ecumenical meetings at Geneva provided the Orthodox Church leaders with a platform for the announcement of their programme. The Orthodox churches had been invited to participate in the preliminary meeting for the World Conference of Faith and Order, and nearly all of them had sent delegates,[9] numbering seventeen in all. These seventeen delegates met in private before the general meeting and decided to follow a common line. The Metropolitan of Seleukia, Germanos, who represented the Ecumenical Patriarchate, acted as their spokesman.

Further, just before the preliminary meeting of Faith and Order, Metropolitan Germanos, accompanied by the Metropolitan of Nubia, Nicolaos, and Archimandrite Papadopoulos, paid a brief visit to the preliminary meeting on Life and Work which was also being held in Geneva. Archbishop Söderblom had invited them so that the Life and Work delegates could learn that the Ecumenical Patriarchate was ready to cooperate with the other churches.

It was at this impromptu meeting that the Encyclical met for the first time with the kind of eager response which the Patriarchate had hoped. In the words of Metropolitan Germanos: "The well-known leader of the ecumenical movement, the late Archbishop of Uppsala, Dr Söderblom, studied and understood the spirit of the above Encyclical... Holding the Encyclical in his hand, he addressed the representatives of the Orthodox Church, emphasizing the existing similarities between the Encyclical and the new plan, and proposed that the Orthodox Church be invited to participate in the preparation."[10]

The Faith and Order meeting provided an opportunity for a fuller exposition of the plan for a League of Churches. There it was made clear that the proposals in the Encyclical were supported by all the Orthodox churches represented at the Faith and Order meeting. Metropolitan Germanos explained that the Orthodox Church, and in particular the Ecumenical Patriarchate, had resolved to send brotherly greetings to all the churches of Christ throughout the world and to invite them to cooperate in a league of churches. At the very moment they had made that decision, they received the invitation to participate in the World Conference on Faith and Order.

Professor Alivisatos of Athens submitted to the meeting the following programme drawn up by the Orthodox Church:

League of Churches
1. To stop proselytizing between the Christian churches, and to promote mutual understanding between them for Christian missions among non-Christian peoples.

2. Help and mutual love of the Christian churches.

3. Association and collaboration of the churches for the purpose of establishing Christian principles and collaboration against every system working against these principles.

4. Knowledge and study by the churches of each other.

5. Reunion of the smaller related Christian communions.

6. Abdication of the churches of all political questions.

7. Examination of *differences of faith and order* in a friendly spirit.

8. Union of all the churches on faith and order as the final purpose of the League of Churches.

Organization of the League of Churches

1. Appointment of a central *permanent* committee of the League of Churches for the accomplishment of the aforesaid purposes.

2. Appointment of special committees in every church which is a member of the League of Churches for the purpose of mutual understanding, and to cooperate with the central committee for that object.

3. Foundation of a special central magazine of the League of Churches for the purpose of mutual understanding, and to cooperate with the central committee for that object.

4. Appointment of several congresses for the above purposes, whose time and place will be fixed by the central committee of the League of Churches.

5. Fixing of time and place of the first World Christian Congress.[11]

The business committee of the meeting noted these proposals, but it was made clear that the Faith and Order Conference would deal only with those aspects concerned with doctrine and church order.

In that same year, Metropolitan Germanos visited Sweden. In a lecture given at Uppsala, after describing the proposals of the Church at Constantinople, he said:

Fortunately, those are not thoughts coming only from Constantinople. Already before the World War, and even so much more after the war, Christians here and there in the Christian world had come to the deep insight that Christendom would lose most of its own authority as long as the Christian churches continued to deal with the questions of common interest for the whole of Christendom in a spirit of disunity and quarrel. The deep acknowledgment of this has, in many ways, given itself expression in an endeavour towards unity, both in dogmatic questions and in questions of a practical nature. I am particularly happy that the latest named endeavour — towards common concepts and cooperation in practical questions — is the concern also of the Swedish Church Primus, Archbishop Nathan Söderblom and, together with him, the Swedish Church.[12]

In 1925, at the Life and Work conference in Stockholm, the plan to form a League of Churches was not mentioned in the addresses or reports. Those responsible for proposing a continuation of that discussion had decided that the time was not yet ripe for the formation of a permanent organization. Two years later, at the Lausanne conference on Faith and Order, the idea of a League of Churches was considered very seriously. The report on "The Unity of Christendom and the Relation thereto of Existing Churches" states that, pending a solution of the questions of faith and order, it was possible for the churches to unite in activities of brotherly service, and mentioned specifically the proposal of the Ecumenical Patriarchate for a League of Churches. It asked the churches to consider what steps were immediately practicable to give effective expression to their unity in service. Thus a very representative ecumenical gathering had recognized that the plan of the Patriarchate indicated the road which the churches had to take if they were to advance towards the goal of unity.

After the Lausanne Conference, then, Archbishop Germanos could say:

> Lastly, Lausanne strengthened in us the thought, which in the last few years had dominated the Ecumenical Patriarchate, relative to the foundation of orthodoxy. This thought is that, in every attempt at reunion of the churches, there must come first the understanding and cooperation between the churches on the points upon which they agree with one another. I do not think that Stockholm with its conference on Life and Work did say the last word in this matter. The establishment of a sort of League of Churches is of pre-eminent value and utility. The rights of every church must be recognized and propaganda among Christians must cease. The signs of love and help to the churches which are unable to fulfill their duties to their own people must prevail. In the same way the churches must unite themselves in contending against the external enemies of Christendom and against the subversive power in its midst. When this league is realized and the reunion of the churches in faith begins with those churches which are holding to the same principles, then it is easier to come to a general reunion according to the words of our Lord: "There shall be one flock and one shepherd."[13]

2. A prediction of J.H. Oldham

It is remarkable that in that same summer of 1920 and in the same place, Geneva, where the proposals for a league of churches or an ecumenical council of churches were presented at the meetings of Life and Work and Faith and Order, a gathering of missionary leaders was held, at which it was predicted that the international missionary organization which they were setting up would lead to the formation of a world league of churches. This prophetic statement was made by Dr J.H. Oldham. After having prepared the World Missionary Conference of 1910 in Edinburgh, he had served as its secretary and had been invited to become the secretary of its continuation committee.

The establishment of this committee was a crucial step for two reasons. It was the first time that an international body was formed in which Christian leaders of different confessions and nations met together, not as individuals, but as representatives of their churches and missionary societies. Equally important was the fact that the continuation committee was given a full-time secretary and an adequate budget. Oldham used to say that in recognizing that an office, a secretariat and a budget were indispensable instruments of effective cooperation, the World Missionary Conference of 1910 anticipated the League of Nations by eight years.

Until 1914, the Continuation Committee was able to carry out its task. During World War I, however, Oldham had to concern himself with the acute problems which it had created for the missionary societies. After the war, it became clear that a new beginning had to be made. In 1920, a special meeting was held at the Château de Crans, near Geneva, at which the thirty-nine delegates were the guests of Colonel and Madame van Berchem. The purpose of this meeting was to decide on the future form of international missionary cooperation.

It is noteworthy that, in a memorandum which he prepared on the subject, Oldham placed the problem of missionary cooperation in the setting of worldwide cooperation among the churches, in line with the thinking of the Edinburgh conference. That conference had assembled not only the specialists concerned with foreign missions but also a very considerable number of leaders of those churches which had established missionary boards. Thus many church leaders had begun to participate in ecumenical activities long before the Stockholm conference of 1925, which is generally considered as the first ecumenical conference because it was composed entirely of delegates who were the representatives of churches. The calling of the church to mission was one of the main themes of the conference. The Archbishop of Canterbury said in his address: "It is my simple thought tonight that the place of missions in the life of the church must be the central place, and none other." Of missionary societies, the conference stated: "The missionary societies are the standard-bearers of the churches as they advance with the gospel of Christ for the conquest of the world."

In his memorandum of 1920, Oldham wrote: "The first question to be determined is whether the international organization should be one of missionary societies and boards or should be, at any rate in part, a league of churches. There appear to be three reasons why the possibility of establishing some direct link with churches as distinct from missionary societies or boards should be considered. First, an arrangement of this nature would best meet existing conditions, in some, at least, of the leading Christian bodies. Secondly, the growing importance of the churches in the mission field is a factor which needs to be taken into account. Thirdly, in matters in which the weight of Christian public opinion needs to be brought to bear, action by church authorities may be more effective than action by missionary boards."

After analyzing the various possibilities, Oldham came however to the conclusion that it might be best to start with an international organization representing the home bases of missions. But he added: "It is becoming less and less possible to discuss missionary matters without representatives of the churches in the mission field, and any organization that may be created will probably have before long to give way to something that may represent the beginning of a world league of churches.''

Was this reference to a league of churches an echo of the proposals made a year earlier by Söderblom and a few months before that by the Ecumenical Patriarchate? When I asked Oldham this question in 1952 he said: ''It is highly improbable that anything I wrote at that time had any connection with statements by the Ecumenical Patriarchate or Archbishop Söderblom. I was not at the time following ecumenical church movements.'' It is surprising to us today, when news of ecumenical affairs is quickly disseminated, that Oldham knew nothing about these other plans. As we have seen, however, the Constantinople Encyclical reached only a small number of church leaders, and Söderblom's plan had not yet been given serious consideration.

Oldham used the expression ''league of churches'' because in those days he was profoundly interested in the process whereby the League of Nations had come into being in January 1920. He was in touch with the ''Round Table'' group, in particular with Lionel Curtis and Philip Kerr, later Lord Lothian, both of whom had taken an active part in the elaboration of the plan for a League of Nations, Curtis as a member of the Peace Delegation at Versailles and Kerr as Lloyd George's private secretary. Both men were also in close touch with General Smuts and Lord Robert Cecil. On 20 September 1952, Oldham wrote to me: ''The Round Table group were my great educators in matters of *constitutional principle*. They clarified my thinking in these matters. I saw clearly that though the Continuation Committee was an organization of church *boards* it was in principle an entirely new development *in church life* and that it might lead in the future to new relations *between the churches themselves*, though I was at the time much too much occupied with IMC post-war problems to look further ahead.''

At the meeting in Crans, there was no discussion regarding a possible league of churches. One participant, Dr Karl Fries of Sweden, a friend of Söderblom, raised the question of future relations between the international missionary organization and the proposed ecumenical conference. However, as I was informed in 1952 by Miss Betty Gibson, who was responsible for the notes taken at the meeting, these show that this point was not taken up.

Oldham did not know at the time that some fifteen years later he would be called upon to fulfill his own prediction.

3. The proposal of Archbishop Söderblom

Archbishop Söderblom's first public reference to the formation of an ecumenical council of churches was made in April 1919.[1] It was the natural outcome of Söderblom's intensive and tenacious struggle to bring together the churches of the nations involved in the war, to render witness to their common Lord. The churches had participated in the general cacophony of the war years. Where was the voice of *Una Sancta*? The Archbishop had been greatly encouraged by the fact that some individuals and groups had responded to his plans for an international meeting. In the United Kingdom, a Council for Promoting a "Christian Meeting" had been set up, one of its most active leaders being William Temple. In *The Challenge*, of which Temple was the editor, many articles in favour of such a meeting appeared. In one of them, J.P. Malleson made the point that the proposed meeting "might well be a step towards the reunion of Christians which we all long to see, that unity for which Christ prayed. It might even develop into a permanent organ for expressing the mind of the church upon great moral questions." Dean Karlström tells us that when Söderblom read this in 1917, he underlined this passage.[2] Years later he quoted it, showing that it had made a lasting impression on his mind.[3]

As soon as the war was over, Söderblom began to prepare the way for a world conference of churches. In his thinking, however, this conference was not to be an end in itself, but should lead to the establishment of a permanent body, which he called "an Ecumenical Council of Churches" *(Ökumenischer Kirchenrat)*.

He explained the proposal in an article which appeared in *The Contemporary Review* in England and in *Die Eiche* in Germany.[4]

He puts the plan in a wide context. Now that the war is over and a new period of history has begun, it is time to think about the world task of Christianity. That task is first of all to manifest the universal character of the Church itself. It is furthermore to work for reconciliation, unity and peace in the relations between nations. The League of Nations will only be an empty shell unless it is filled with the Christian spirit.

We need an evangelical catholicity which will not demand uniformity but serve and strengthen the cause of spiritual unity. A common organization must be formed, capable of representing Christendom. "What I propose is an ecumenical council, representing the whole of Christendom, and so constructed that it can speak on behalf of Christendom."

For the time being, he went on to say, we cannot expect that Rome will be ready to participate. There remain two ancient offices which have special qualifications to have a place in the council, namely the Patriarchate of Constantinople and the Archbishopric of Canterbury. Then the evangelical-catholic churches should have their representative in the council. The council should not be invested with external authority, but should gain its influence according to the degree in which it would be able to act as a spiritual power. It should speak, not *ex cathedra*, but from the depths of the Christian conscience. The time has come when we may venture to believe in the unity of Christianity and take definite measures to express the same.

A few weeks after writing this article, in September 1919, Söderblom attended the meeting of the World Alliance for Promoting International Friendship through the Churches at Oud Wassenaar, in the Netherlands. This first ecumenical meeting of church leaders after the war seemed to provide an excellent opportunity to get the proposal adopted. So Söderblom submitted a memorandum on the subject.[5] It said:

> 1. Our task is not to bring organizations together, but to unite hearts and minds and endeavours. True believers and followers of Christ have always been a minority even in the Christian communions, and they will ever remain a minority. But it is essential to use for Christian aims all communions of the Church, and all Christian organizations to which it is our privilege to belong.
>
> Our ecumenical conference has to be clearly distinguished from the great task that is called the World Conference on Faith and Order. The commission sent to Europe for that world conference quite agreed with

us in that respect. Our conference may be a most important preparation for the World Conference on Faith and Order, but it will not deal with Faith nor Order, but (with) some well-defined urgent practical aims.

Union for such purposes does not require unity in Faith and Order. I remind you of the doctrine in the Augsburg Confession and the Thirty-nine Articles in that respect. Dr Carrolls renders the same doctrine in his Primer on Church Unity, answer 49. Uniformity is not necessary for common preaching and striving in actual needs of mankind. The report of the Archbishop's Fifth Questionnaire says (page 2): We say deliberately that in the region of moral or social questions we desire all Christians to begin at once to act together as if they were one body in one visible fellowship. This could be done by all alike without any injury to theological principles.

I have tried to define the chief objects of the ecumenical conference in an article which appeared some weeks ago in *The Contemporary Review*, London. They seem to me to be: (a) common doctrine and endeavour for international Christian brotherhood and organized unity of nations; (b) Christian principles and action for social renewal of society; further (c) a common voice must be created for the Christian conscience. I advocate an ecumenical council representing Christendom in a spiritual way.

2. As to the comprehensiveness of this proposed gathering, good reasons speak for beginning with Evangelical Christendom only, in order to create a common platform for our part of the Catholic church before inviting the Orthodox and Roman divisions of the Church.

But there are also good reasons and warm sympathies for making the scope as comprehensive as possible at once.

3. As to the place of the conference my brethren in Copenhagen and Christiania and myself have the honour of reiterating our invitation to one of the Scandinavian countries.

As we read the article and the memorandum we note that the article speaks about the plan to create a "council" and that the memorandum speaks about a "conference" except in the one sentence which says with considerable emphasis: "I advocate an ecumenical council representing Christendom in a spiritual way." I take this to mean that Söderblom was most eager to get the idea of a permanent council accepted but that he realized that it would be wise to begin with proposing the world conference.

In fact the meeting at Oud Wassenaar which had its hands full with the task of reconstructing the World Alliance did not give much attention to Söderblom's memorandum. It said about the world conference that "such a conference, if it can be arranged, will prove an inestimable blessing to mankind". It did not, however, express any opinion regarding the idea of an "ecumenical council".

It is also noteworthy that in the article Söderblom speaks of the Ecumenical Patriarchate of Constantinople as one of the two "ancient offices" which will be represented in the council, but that in the memorandum he speaks of the question of the participation of the Orthodox churches as an open question. This means, as his action in 1920 shows, that he knew of the desire of some Protestants to create a purely Protestant body and waited for the opportunity to get the wider ecumenical conception accepted.

We can summarize this plan in the following way: (a) there was need for a permanent organ of the churches; (b) it was to be the voice of the Christian conscience; (c) it had to be truly representative; (d) it was not to claim jurisdictional but only spiritual authority; (e) it had to be as universal as possible; (f) its composition would be based partly on *ex officio* membership and partly on election.

In the summer of 1920, it became possible, through the common efforts of the Federal Council of Churches in the United States of America, the Swiss Federation of Churches and Söderblom, to hold in Geneva the preparatory meeting for the Universal Christian Conference on Life and Work. There Söderblom again urged that the conference should create a permanent body. In the "suggested programme" which he brought with him he stated:

> The Conference must not pass without creating definitive organizations: an ecumenical council was to be formed, "consisting of a number of representatives of Christendom, of whom some were to be chosen *ad hoc* in the broadest democratic way by the Christian communions, some selected among leaders of important offices in the Christian church. This ecumenical council which ought to have its official seat in Jerusalem or another historical place of our Christian faith, should constitute a purely spiritual authority, without any mandate to interfere in internal church affairs".

The pencil notes for Archbishop Söderblom's introductory address contained the phrase: "We must have an *ecumenical council.*"

Söderblom had been greatly encouraged by the Encyclical of the Ecumenical Patriarchate, issued at the beginning of 1920. Its proposal concerning a league of churches was very similar to his own for a council of churches. He therefore wanted the Orthodox to support his plan at Geneva. They had however not been invited to the Life and Work meeting because the question as to whether Life and Work should embrace all churches or only the Protestant churches had not yet been settled. Orthodox delegates had however come to Geneva to attend the meeting on Faith and Order. Söderblom could not let this opportunity pass. On the one hand, he could show the supporters of a pan-Protestant world conference that the Eastern churches were ready to join in an ecumenical movement of all the churches. On the other, by calling attention to the Encyclical from Constantinople he could show that his idea of an ecumenical council was not as strange as it had seemed to many. He therefore took it upon himself to invite three Orthodox church leaders to the Life and Work meeting. Their spokesman was Metropolitan Germanos with whom Söderblom had been acquainted since the World Student Christian Federation meeting in Istanbul in 1911.

We have already quoted from Metropolitan Germanos's description of this encounter.[6] Söderblom obviously enjoyed this exercise in accelerating the course of church history, for he wrote to his young friend, J. Kolmodin, who served as his liaison with the Ecumenical Patriarchate of Constantinople: "The question of whether we were going to accept the Greeks was rather critical. I presented the conference with a *fait accompli* in simply inviting the Greeks to proceed into the hall where they were solemnly welcomed — which all parties afterwards fully approved."

In the sober language of the official record it is stated that immediately after the visit of the Eastern Orthodox church leaders, Bishop Cannon of the United States moved "that the Committee of Arrangements be instructed to invite all Christian communions to participate in the proposed conference". After discussion, this motion was adopted.

This was a decision which was to have far-reaching consequences. It meant that Life and Work would not become a pan-Protestant movement, as some had envisaged, but that it would seek to include the Eastern Orthodox churches as well as the Church of England which had no desire to join an exclusively Protestant organization. Further, since Faith and Order had from its beginnings in 1910 invited all churches which accepted its Christological basis to participate in the movement, Life and Work and Faith and Order had from the 1920 meeting onwards the same constituency. This obliged the two movements to cooperate, and thus the way was prepared for the realization of the plans for a permanent council, as they had been conceived in Constantinople and Uppsala.

But there was to be another consequence. The churches which were ready to take part in the ecumenical adventure now decided not to take the easy path of creating a body with a membership of churches which had more or less similar doctrinal and ecclesiological positions. They chose the far more difficult task of forming a movement in which there would be deep tensions as churches, which had lived in separation for a thousand years and had developed their own processes of thought and styles of life, tried to enter into fellowship with one another. How difficult that was to be was not fully realized in those early days. That was to become clear some thirty years later, when the movement had to define its understanding of itself.

4. World Conference on Life and Work, Stockholm 1925

From 1920 to 1925, the years of preparation for the Stockholm Conference on Life and Work, Archbishop Söderblom continued to emphasize that the most important and urgent task ahead was the formation of a permanent and representative body to speak for the Christian churches. He described his ecumenical programme in a book, *Christian Fellowship*, which appeared in English in 1923, and in German in 1925 under the title *Einigung der Christenheit*. In this work, he stated that the establishment of such a permanent ecumenical council was "impatiently" and "most generally" desired. He assured his readers that "the Universal Christian Conference will create such a common speaking-trumpet".[1]

As we turn to the report of the Stockholm conference, therefore, we might expect to find that Söderblom had used this unique occasion to convince the delegates that nothing was more urgent than the creation of such a permanent council. To our surprise, however, we find that he made no reference to his great plan during the conference. The conference adopted the report which proposed the setting up of a continuation committee of the conference, but stated clearly: "The commission deems it inexpedient and beyond the proper jurisdiction of the conference to attempt to form any authoritative or permanent organization."[2] It is of particular interest that the motion to approve the report was presented by Archbishop Germanos. He could have used the conference as a platform from which to develop Constantinople's proposal for a league of churches, which was not yet widely known. However, he did not mention the idea, and even stated explicitly that what was needed was a continuation committee and not a permanent body.

How do we explain this apparent change in the attitude of the two chief protagonists of the idea for a council? They still cherished the vision, but they had realized that it could only be realized in stages, of which the first was obviously the successful completion of the Stockholm Conference. They had discovered to their surprise that the plan for a permanent council would be a handicap and not a help in obtaining agreement among the delegates. Charles S. MacFarland has written that some church representatives, particularly the American Lutherans, had come to Stockholm "almost on condition that no continuing organization should be set up".[3] Anglican hesitation concerning a council in which the Roman Catholic Church would not be represented had not been fully overcome. The German position was stated at Stockholm by Dr Scholz, the former chief court chaplain and "Oberkonsistorialrat", who was obviously thinking of plans such as those elaborated at Constantinople and Uppsala when he said: "It would be an artificial action to create today a world-embracing league of churches *(Kirchenbund)* which would tend to ignore the sixteen-hundred year old Confessional churches and have no understanding of the will of God and his ways."[4]

There is also evidence that Söderblom's proposal to reserve permanent seats for "ancient offices in the church", such as the Patriarchate of Constantinople and the Archbishopric of Canterbury, while other seats would be filled by election for a certain period, had created the suspicion that the plan would lead to domination by the older national churches. MacFarland reports that "the Archbishop's plan was deemed slightly hierarchical, involving a council which to some looked almost papal".[5] There was one speaker, however, who had positive and wise words to say for the council. George Bell, then Dean of Canterbury, said:

> It would be inexpedient, the report of the Fifth Commission declares, to attempt at this moment to form any authoritative or permanent organization. I can conceive very great gains from an international Christian council which in certain grave questions, or in certain grave emergencies, could genuinely focus the considered opinion of all the churches (or of all save one great church), and could in its action or judgment have the general public opinion of the churches behind it at a particular time. But the creation of such a council, and the winning by it of the confidence of the churches, must take time.
>
> In particular I would say that (in addition to the right spiritual motive at its back) there are four conditions indispensable to its success: (1) It

should know exactly the work it is to do. (2) It should have thoroughly adequate funds. (3) It should have the secure, if gradual, support of the constituent churches. For it will be on the churches at large, and not on leading individuals, that its authority will rest. (4) It should have the absolutely right man as its secretary — a man very hard to find, but on the finding of whom, more than on any other human factor, the value of the council would depend.[6]

If Söderblom was disappointed, he did not show it. With his usual optimism, he wrote: "Thus the beginning is made for an ecumenical council, however one would prefer to name such a common organ for Christendom, empowered with purely spiritual authority, but capable of speaking and acting whenever needed."[7]

5. World Conference on Faith and Order, Lausanne 1927

In 1927 the first World Conference on Faith and Order was held at Lausanne. Since it was to deal exclusively with the issues of doctrine and the constitution of the church, it was not expected that there would be discussion of the Constantinople proposal for a league of churches dealing mainly with social and moral problems, or of Söderblom's similar plan. In fact, they became the subject of a sharp conflict, perhaps the most serious which the conference had to face.

This was due largely to the way in which Söderblom used his position as chairman of the seventh section, which dealt with "the unity of Christendom and relation thereto of the existing churches". Judging by his prudent diplomacy at the Stockholm conference, and his self-restraint there on the subject of the council plan, it was expected that he would take the same line at the Lausanne Faith and Order conference two years later. If he had not been able to get sufficient backing for it at a meeting where he was the host and had a position of tremendous influence, he could not hope to be more successful at a world meeting of a movement in which he had not played an important role, and where some considered him as the leader of a competing organization. It is true that he had been a member of the Faith and Order Committee set up in Geneva in 1920, but he had not taken an active part in the preparation for the Lausanne conference. In spite of these handicaps, he went straight ahead with the advocacy of his plan for a council. The paragraph which he wrote for the report of the Commission is easily recognized as coming from him. It read:

In fulfilling the Master's law of love all Christians should act together as if they were one body in one visible fellowship without any injury to theological principles. In 1920, the Ecumenical Patriarchate issued to Christendom an Encyclical Letter proposing a *koinonia ton ekklesion*, a league of churches for practical purposes, without authority to commit the churches. It was followed up by the Universal Christian Conference on Life and Work (Stockholm 1925). This work must be continued and strengthened, and will surely prepare the way for fuller spiritual unity through faith in God and our Lord Jesus Christ, the faith underlying and inspiring all Christian life and work. A council of churches for practical purposes might be well evolved from already existing organizations such as the Continuation Committee on Life and Work, consisting of representatives officially appointed by almost all Christian communions, and the International Committee of the World Alliance for Promoting International Friendship through the Churches.[1]

This however meant asking for the unqualified backing of the Faith and Order movement for the creation of an ecumenical organ which emphasized the common practical task rather than the achievement of full unity in faith and order. The council could be seen as an attempt "to substitute the half-way house of federation for the ideal of organic union".[2] Moreover, the "as if" formula which Söderblom had found in an Anglican report and which he used very frequently, as in the above statement, could also lead to serious misunderstanding.[3] Did Life and Work only pretend to have unity? Had not Söderblom spoken with gratitude of a unity found at Stockholm, and which, though very imperfect and incomplete, was nevertheless *real*?

When the first draft of the commission report was presented by Söderblom, the paragraph quoted above was not criticized. The second draft was presented in his absence, when he had left Lausanne to keep a previous appointment. On this occasion, a small group of American Anglo-Catholics attacked the report sharply, in particular the paragraph drafted by Söderblom. In order to safeguard the principle of *nemine contradicente*, Bishop Brent proposed that the question be referred to the continuation committee for such consideration as it was competent to give, and this motion was carried. The continuation committee appointed a group, with the Bishop of Gloucester as convener, to prepare a revised draft of section seven. Their text was adopted by the business committee of Faith and Order in December 1927, and submitted to the churches for their consideration. As for the main differences between the two texts, the new text left out the "as if" motivation and the propagandistic phrase about Life and Work. It maintained the statement about a "league or council for practical purposes", as a possible solution to the problem of interchurch relations, but it added that there was a difference of opinion as to whether such a council should include Life and Work only, or also Faith and Order.

6. A universal Christian council for Life and Work

The promoters of the council plan had good reason to feel encouraged. The proposal to form a permanent organization had not been rejected at Lausanne. Söderblom felt therefore that the time had come to take decisive action. His conviction, his tenacity, perhaps also the feeling that he had little time to carry out what he saw as a God-given mandate, made him return to the attack. The appearance of the encyclical *Mortalium Animos* in 1928 helped indirectly to make Söderblom's plan more acceptable. The sharp refusal by the Vatican to accept any kind of interchurch fellowship meant, for those Anglicans and Orthodox who had so far hesitated about the formation of a council without Roman participation, that they could no longer maintain that waiting for Rome was a realistic alternative.

In May 1928, therefore, Söderblom turned to his comrade-in-arms, Metropolitan Germanos, who was chairman of the continuation committee of Life and Work for that year, and implored him to use this position to advance their common goal. He wrote to the Metropolitan:

> The really ecumenical initiative for a new epoch of cooperation and unity in the Church and in Christendom came from the Ecumenical Patriarchate in Constantinople, 1920, that is certainly from you. Would not the time be ripe now for you to propose such a federation or league of churches? You have the kernel in the continuation committee over which you preside yourself. Besides we have the World Alliance, the International Missionary Council, which has become, I am glad to say, eager to have also the Orthodox Church represented. Further, there is the continuation committee of Faith and Order. Can you not propose to the

Executive Committee on Life and Work to invite a few men to come together and propose lines and rules for such a federation? In several cases, as with regard to yourself, the same man represents his church in two or three or even in some cases in all four of those strivings and organizations for cooperation and unity. Such a federation would of course be most clearly distinguished from a real church unity, a reunited church, an organic unity, but as you said at Lausanne, and as you have explained on different occasions, federation is the first step and a necessary step. If such a committee could be entrusted in Prague with proposing and outlining the scheme of an ecumenical church federation, it is not excluded that the Ecumenical Patriarchate of Constantinople and Christendom can celebrate in 1930 the pastoral letter of 1920 on a league of churches, with the formation of such a koinonia.[1]

At the meeting of the continuation committee of Life and Work at Eisenach in 1929 it was proposed "to constitute the Stockholm movement as a permanent organization" and to give it the name "Universal Christian Council for Life and Work" (Conseil œcuménique du Christianisme pratique — Ökumenischer Rat für Praktisches Christentum). This proposal was accepted and, at its next session, at Chexbres in 1930, the last meeting which Söderblom attended before his death in 1931, the continuation committee adopted a constitution for the new body, which included these names.

A Universal Christian Council for Life and Work had thus come into being, but this did not mean that the plans conceived at Constantinople and Uppsala had been realized. When Father Pribilla wrote in 1931 that Söderblom's dream had remained a utopia, Söderblom replied that it was not wholly utopian, since the continuation committee of Life and Work had, at Chexbres, become the Universal Christian Council for Life and Work.[2] But his use of the words "not wholly" *(doch nicht ganz)* shows that, although the name of the new body, especially in its French and German forms, seemed to correspond to his proposal of 1919, the Council was in reality only a pale reflection of his idea.

It is true that the constitution of 1930 contains some features of Söderblom's original proposal. The article on "Officers" for example states that the presidents of the five sections should be nominated by their section, and that these nominations should be confirmed by the council. However, this is followed by a note to the effect that, until otherwise determined, the president of the Orthodox section would be the Ecumenical Patriarch, and the president of the British section would be the Archbishop of Canterbury, who would each take the chair for two years. Söderblom's principle of giving a special place to two "ancient offices" thus received constitutional sanction. In most other respects, however, an adequate response to the challenge issued in Oud Wassenaar in 1919 and in Constantinople in 1920 was not given at Chexbres in 1930.

A serious weakness of the new Council was that it had not received a clear mandate from the churches. The constitutional anomaly was that a continuation committee set up on the understanding that it would not create a permanent body had declared itself to *be* a permanent body, and this without having obtained the approval of the churches. Further, the problem of the representation of the churches had not been solved. According to its constitution, the Council consisted of five sections, representing the Orthodox Church, Continental European churches, British churches, American churches and churches not otherwise included. These sections were however rather nebulous bodies. In his chairman's address in 1932, Bishop Bell said: "In fact, what has happened is, with one or two exceptions, that the sections have not had a really definite and systematic church organization on which they could be built up." Since the churches had not been asked to accept full responsibility for the new Council, they had no sense of commitment to it. An additional point of weakness was that the Council did not have a full-time general secretary, and shared its general secretariat with the World Alliance for Friendship through the Churches. Moreover, the problem of the coordination of the various ecumenical movements had not been solved. In the address just quoted, Bishop Bell said: "The variety of expression is most baffling to the mass of churchmen. It increases the difficulty of making an international appeal to the different churches."

The fundamental problem was that of the relation of Life and Work to Faith and Order. Could Life and Work or, as the French and German titles had it "practical Christianity", really give adequate guidance in the field of social and international life if it remained only practical? And if it concerned itself with the underlying theological and doctrinal issues, was it not in fact entering into the territory of Faith and Order? For the sake of a healthy development of the ecumenical movement these questions required a clear answer.

7. A new departure in time of crisis: W. A. Brown's initiative

The economic and financial crisis which followed the crash of 1929 created almost insuperable difficulties for all international organizations. The ecumenical bodies were especially vulnerable because they were also facing an internal crisis which, by 1932, had become the main theme of ecumenical discussion.

At the Life and Work meeting of 1932, Prof. Runestam of Sweden opened his address with these words: "The crisis of the ecumenical movement, which is the subject of so many discussions, is the crisis of the ecumenical movement as a whole."[1] In addition to problems of organization and structure, there was the vital question of the identity and *raison d'être* of the movement.

The need for structural improvement was obvious. There were, in fact, two structural problems. One, as we have seen, was the relationship of the ecumenical bodies to the churches. Though all these bodies claimed to represent the churches, none was effectively rooted in and clearly accountable to them. The churches therefore were not ready to accept full responsibility for the activities carried on by the ecumenical organizations.

Another problem was the multiplicity of existing ecumenical bodies; there were too many different bodies working towards unity and cooperation, and it was not easy to integrate them. Indeed many church leaders were active in several of them, but in each were also the diehards who refused to give up their total independence. Some members of Life and Work feared that theological debates would distract the movement from its prophetic action in the world. Some in Faith and Order felt that Life and Work was concerned with worldly affairs, and was not sufficiently concerned with the visible unity of the church. For example, in 1933, Life and Work approached Faith and Order with a proposal to appoint a liaison group. Ralph W. Brown, till that year secretary of Faith and Order, proposed to his executive committee to reply to the suggestion of appointing what he called "a supercommittee of the two movements" by pointing out that Faith and Order had decided in 1929 that cooperation between the two bodies should be confined for the time being to a friendly relationship, and could therefore not respond to the proposal of Life and Work.

A first step towards coordination had been taken in 1932 when Life and Work and the World Alliance for Promoting International Friendship through the Churches appointed Henry Louis Henriod as general secretary of both bodies. This however did not solve the basic problem, as the World Alliance was not, in most countries, officially related to, or responsible to, the churches. Moreover, the really important issue was the relationship between Life and Work and Faith and Order. In this connection, a far-reaching initiative was taken in 1933 by William Adams Brown of New York. He had played a leading role both in the Stockholm conference of Life and Work and in that of Faith and Order in Lausanne. Further, he had contacts with the International Missionary Movement and the World Alliance, and had become chairman of the administrative committee of Life and Work in 1932. On sabbatical leave in 1933, he travelled extensively in Europe, where he found a strong desire among church leaders for an integrated ecumenical movement. He therefore asked the Archbishop of York, William Temple, to invite a small group of responsible people from the various ecumenical organizations to spend a few days together at Bishopthorpe.

The group which thus came together consisted of William Temple and H.N. Bate for Faith and Order, William Adams Brown and Samuel McCrea Cavert for Life and Work, Valdemar Ammundsen and Henry Louis Henriod for the World Alliance, J.H. Oldham and William Paton for the International Missionary Council, Charles Guillon for the YMCA and I myself for the World Student Christian Federation. As we surveyed together the ecumenical scene, we found little reason to hope for a speedy solution of the problems in the way of simplification and unification. Even in the short time of their existence, each organization had developed its own ethos, style and constituency. We agreed however that fundamentally we were working towards the same goal, seeing one another as members of a team moving in the same direction, and not as competitors. The resolution we adopted was later approved by the various responsible committees. It stated:

> Recognizing that the church for its own service to the world needs the ecclesiastical approach to the problems of unity represented by Faith and Order, the practical approach represented by Life and Work, the World Alliance and the IMC and the general impulse towards unity represented by the World Youth movements, and further that each of the three types should therefore be maintained in distinctness, we yet also consider that they are dealing with a situation which can only be understood in its totality; we are agreed in regarding it as vitally important that those mainly concerned in the direction of these movements should meet regularly and maintain consultation with one another, so as to facilitate the rendering of mutual assistance.

In the following years, the unofficial consultative group formed at York met often. It had not yet taken a definite stand for any particular plan of reorganization, but several of the members made no secret of their conviction that reorganization was an urgent necessity, and that it should take the form of a league or an ecumenical council proposed by the pioneers. In his report to the executive committee of Life and Work in Novi Sad in 1933, William Adams Brown spoke of the visits which he had paid to many churches in his capacity as chairman of the administrative committee of Life and Work. In Constantinople, he had been received by the Ecumenical Patriarch, who had repeated the proposal of 1920, saying that the goal was a representative council of the churches which would meet at regular intervals. In his report, Prof. Brown stressed that no better objective could be found than the creation of such a council.

Slowly but surely, the number of advocates for the plan of an integrated council increased. The youth group at the Faith and Order meeting at Hertenstein in 1934 voted in favour of "a World Council for Ecumenical Christianity". It was hoped by many that in 1937, a year when two world conferences would be held, the time would be ripe for a new approach to the problem of ecumenical structure.

8. J. H. Oldham takes the lead

The solution of the problem of structure depended, however, on a clarification of the nature of the ecumenical movement. The younger generation in particular was demanding a more convincing interpretation of the purpose of the movement. These young people lived in a climate very different from that of 1925 and 1927, when the earlier conferences had been held. The optimism of the Social Gospel and the enthusiasm for the League of Nations had vanished, and the liberal theology which had dominated the 1920s was under severe attack from the dialectical theologians. In 1932, the young Dietrich Bonhoeffer spoke for many of his contemporaries when he asked whether the ecumenical movement was a manifestation of a new awareness of the calling of the church, or only an undertaking of a practical and organizational nature. If it were the first, he said, it had to produce a clear theology, a definite conception of the God-given mission of the church. He then asked: "Do we have such a conception?"[1]

Fortunately, from many quarters came contributions to the renewal of the church's understanding of itself. In the field of New Testament studies, it was again recognized that the creation of the *Ekklesia* as the Body of Christ and the People of God was an essential part of the *kerygma*, the message of the gospel. In other branches of theology also there was a rediscovery of the church. In 1934, in its Declaration of Barmen, the German Confessing Church said: "The Christian Church is the congregation of brethren in which Jesus Christ acts presently as the Lord in Word and Sacrament through the Holy Spirit. As the church of pardoned sinners it has to testify in the midst of a sinful world, with its faith as with its obedience, with its message as with its order, that it is solely his property, and that it lives and wants to live solely from his comfort and from his direction in the expectation of his appearance." That strong affirmation was written by Karl Barth. It represented however not only the conviction of the school of dialectical theology to which he belonged, but also that of many other theologians inside and outside Germany. At the same time in fact, Eastern Orthodox theology with its strong ecclesiology began to attract the attention of Western theologians, and Anglican theology made a similar contribution.

It was not by accident, however, that the statement which we have just quoted was included in a document produced during a struggle in which the very life of the Church as the Church of Christ was at stake. There was little doubt that the attempt of totalitarian governments to make the Church subservient to absolute nationalism and the state obliged the churches to rediscover and restate their fundamental calling. In this way, the church conflict in Germany stimulated in the whole ecumenical movement a concentration on the nature of the Church. As a result, the officers of Life and Work decided in 1933 to hold a special meeting in the following year on "The Church and the Problem of the State". This meeting, prepared by Dr Schönfeld and Dr Ehrenström, was held in Paris under the chairmanship of Pastor Boegner. It was attended by Max Huber of the Permanent Court of International Justice, Nicolas Berdyaev, the Russian philosopher, J.H. Oldham of the International Missionary Council, and a number of leading theologians, and there a thorough analysis was made of the new problems which the Church had to face. Further attention was given to these questions in the summer of 1934, at the session of Life and Work held at Fanö. There the chairman, Bishop George Bell, said in his introductory address:

> Every generation is called to do its own rethinking of Christian fundamentals. For us that rethinking, it seems pretty clear, may most appropriately centre on the functions of the Christian Church in, and its relations to, the modern state. We have indeed in our own movement been driven to see the centrality of this issue with particular force by the concrete example of the new German National Socialist State in its relations with the Evangelical Church (as well as with the Roman Catholic Church). The problems which the German Evangelical Church is facing have a vital interest for the whole of Christendom.

At this meeting, Dr Oldham was appointed chairman of the advisory committee on research and it was proposed that the theme of the next world conference should be "Church, Community and State". From that moment until the Utrecht Conference of 1938, Oldham was the central figure in the Life and Work movement and held the most strategic position in the ecumenical movement as a whole.

Some explanation is perhaps needed regarding Oldham's sudden emergence as a leader of Life and Work. He gave his reasons in a letter to John R. Mott, who was not a little disturbed that his old comrade in the missionary movement had now chosen to devote himself almost entirely to an ecclesiastical body. Oldham wrote that the opportunity offered to him was "an unexpected opening for doing what since the meeting at Jerusalem (of the International Missionary Council) I have been trying to do, with a much larger hope of success. Though I was not present at Jerusalem, that meeting had a more profound influence on my thinking and attitude than any other similar experience of my life. The contribution of Rufus Jones opened my eyes to the realities of the world in which we are living.... Consequently, when the Universal Christian Council (for Life and Work) turned to me and appealed for help in the proposed undertaking, I found myself before an opportunity which for years I had been praying and looking for.... Fundamentally (this) is a question of what steps can most effectively be taken to meet one of the gravest situations in the history of the Christian church."[2]

In an "Explanation to the Churches" presented by Oldham to the Fanö meeting and adopted there, he characterized the situation as follows: "No question more urgently demands the grave and earnest consideration of Christian people than the relation between the Church, the state and the community, since on these practical issues is focused the great and critical debate between the Christian faith and the secular tendencies of our time. In this struggle the very existence of the Christian Church is at stake."[3] Oldham was deeply convinced that the churches had to be mobilized for this confrontation and that they had to begin by realizing again that to be a Christian is to be a member of the new society created by God's redeeming act.

With such vigorous leadership, the days of uncertainty for Life and Work were over. The movement again had a definite theme and orientation. Oldham concentrated with extraordinary single-mindedness on this new task. Like Diogenes with his lantern, he went around looking for the right men and women to help in the great undertaking. Like Socrates, he practised "the art of midwifery" by asking those whom he considered as "the ablest minds" to answer vital questions about the crisis of our civilization and the predicament of the church. He was preparing for a world conference, but he was fully aware that it would be irrelevant if it did not lead to a renewal of the life of the churches, and he reflected constantly on the shape which the ecumenical movement should take.

In his writings and contributions to discussions at meetings, we find in the first place that he emphasized that the future organization should be an instrument of the churches, in the sense that it would not be able to act apart from them. He believed that there had been a constitutional ambiguity in Life and Work because its members included not only leading churchmen, appointed by their churches, but also persons who had not been so appointed and who had no voice in the churches' controlling organs. Oldham's insistence on this point was a result not only of his constitutional thinking, but also of his ecclesiological convictions, for, as we have seen, he believed that "the Christian world community" would grow out of the life of the churches. In an article written at the end of his life,[4] he stated that he had supported those with "ecclesiastical sense", although he had never been drawn to ecclesiastical affairs and by temperament had concerned himself more with matters on the frontier beween the church and the world.

In the second place, Oldham desired an ecumenical world organization which would give a very considerable place to the laity. This advocate of ecclesiastical thinking at the same time consistently defended the simple truth, so seldom taken seriously, that in the great confrontation of the churches with the modern world "the layman was more important than the theologian".[5] It was the combination of these two points of emphasis — the one on the church, the other on the laity — that made Oldham's contribution to the debate about the future truly unique.

The third point which he stressed was the importance of study and research, which he emphasized whenever he spoke of the future ecumenical organization, sometimes even calling this its main function. The churches needed the help of the "ablest minds", and the process of common thinking had to be so organized that these could be used to the best advantage.

Thus, under Oldham's leadership, Life and Work gave a considerable place to hard theological thinking. The list of writers of memoranda and of chapters for the preparatory volumes for the Oxford Conference of 1937 includes nearly all theologians who were known as people who had a specific contribution to make. It was no longer possible to say that Life and Work was concerned only with practical problems.

What would this mean for its relations with Faith and Order?

9. William Temple meets American church leaders at Princeton

Archbishop William Temple had close relations with four of the ecumenical bodies. He was convinced that the time had come to give the ecumenical movement a more unified structure and a stronger constitutional basis. Because of his profound interest in the social implications of the Christian faith, he was regarded as a leader in the area of Life and Work, and because of his skill in reconciling theological differences, he had succeeded Bishop Brent as chairman of Faith and Order.

Temple's visit to the United States in 1935 appeared a unique opportunity for involving American church leaders in the discussion started in 1933 at Bishopthorpe under the leadership of Temple himself. Invitations to meet Archbishop Temple at Princeton were therefore sent by Bishop Perry and Dr Leiper to American representatives of Life and Work, Faith and Order, the International Missionary Council, the World Alliance for Friendship through the Churches and the World Student Christian Federation. The purpose was to explore the issues rather than to take decisions. A resolution was however adopted which stated that, as the question of closer relations between the various ecumenical organizations would undoubtedly be considered at the world conferences of Life and Work and Faith and Order to be held in 1937, and at that of the International Missionary Council in 1938, committees should be requested to consider steps to extend the present cooperation, and to regularize the informal consultative group which had been active since the Bishopthorpe meeting of 1933. This recommendation was accepted, and the consultative group was authorized to study possible ways of coordinating the ecumenical movement.

Perhaps the most important aspect of the Princeton meeting was that William Temple made his own position clear; he advocated the creation of "an interdenominational, international council representing all the churches with committees to carry on various projects now forming the objectives of distinct world movements". His plea was for a "thoroughly official council", and a "thoroughly coordinated ecumenical movement". Because of his very great prestige, this lead by Temple was a tremendous encouragement to those who supported the plans for a league or council of churches proposed in 1919 and 1920.

10. Faith and Order considers the next steps towards unity

We have seen that during the 1930s Life and Work was becoming more "theological", while Faith and Order was becoming more "practical". This convergent development was an important factor in bringing the two movements together.

The first World Conference on Faith and Order in 1927 had not been able to give much guidance to the churches regarding the concrete action which they should take to advance the cause of unity. The American members of the F&O continuation committee therefore proposed the creation of a new commission on "an empirical approach to unity", later changed to "the church's unity in life and worship". This commission, under the chairmanship of Dean W.L. Sperry of Harvard University, was composed largely of American churchmen, although some representatives of churches in other countries also participated in its work. It was this commission which put the very concrete issue of "non-theological factors affecting unity" on the ecumenical agenda and made the theologians aware that the divisions between the churches were by no means due only to doctrinal differences, but also, and sometimes to a very high degree, to social or political factors.

At the Lausanne conference there had been considerable resistance to the concept of church federation for cooperative action. Those opposing the idea were afraid that the acceptance of federal relationships might obscure the goal of full unity and delay its realization. The commission expressed the conviction that federations could be, and often were, a promising approach to complete unity.

One of the five reports of the commission on "The Church's Unity in Life and Worship", put into final form by William Adams Brown, dealt with the theme "Next Steps on the Road to a United Church". According to this report, "all were agreed" that some closer coordination of the ecumenical movement was a crying need.[1] The report proposed the "holding at stated intervals, say once in five or ten years, of conferences of official representatives of all the branches of the church now represented in the conferences of Life and Work and Faith and Order and any others who were willing to join for the purpose of unhurried consideration of such topics as were most pressing at the time".[2] The report was published in April 1937, a few months before the conferences of Oxford and Edinburgh were to consider the plan for a world council. It was a remarkable illustration of the evolution in Faith and Order, and showed that the time was ripe for imaginative action for the integration of various parts of the ecumenical movement.

It must be added that the movement's financial situation provided advocates of integration with a further strong argument. At a time of economic crisis, it had become exceedingly difficult to convince the churches that they should support several different ecumenical organizations. At the same time, the leadership of Faith and Order was to a large extent in the hands of the same people as were active in Life and Work. Thus, at the Edinburgh conference of 1937, we find in the committee of arrangements William Temple, Germanos of Thyatira, William Adams Brown, John R. Mott and myself, all of whom had played a leading role in the Life and Work conference at Oxford. It is especially interesting that the man who had become the symbol of Christian action and practical Christianity, John R. Mott, was at this time helping to shape the policy of Faith and Order as chairman of the sub-section considering the next steps to be taken on the road to a united church.

11. The decisive meeting at Westfield College

In the summer of 1936, a meeting of Life and Work was held at Chamby and one of Faith and Order at Clarens. Both meetings approved the appointment of a committee of thirty members, later increased to thirty-five, "to review the work of ecumenical cooperation since the Stockholm and Lausanne conferences and to make recommendations to the Oxford and Edinburgh conferences regarding the future policy, organization and work of the ecumenical movement". The members were to be nominated by the consultative group, and were mainly to be people occupying positions of ecclesiastical responsibility. The views of laymen, women and youth were, however, also to be represented. I was invited to become a member of this committee.

The thirty-five members met at Westfield College in London with only two and a half days, 8-10 July 1937, to accomplish the difficult task. In actual fact that task proved easier than had been expected, because at least ten of the thirty-five had been thinking along these lines. There were Archbishop Germanos and J.H. Oldham, who had been thinking in terms of a league or council as early as 1920. To them could be added Dean (later Archbishop) Brilioth, closely associated with the work of his father-in-law, Archbishop Söderblom, and in complete agreement with Söderblom's plan. Further there were seven of us who had been working together on the question of the future of the ecumenical movement since the Bishopthorpe meeting of 1933.

The first general discussion showed that there was a readiness to take two radical decisions: to bring together Life and Work and Faith and Order and to set up a fully representative assembly of the churches. In the introductory speeches, William Temple and Yngve Brilioth emphasized that the two world conferences provided a unique opportunity for making this new departure. In the discussion, it was generally agreed that a more comprehensive organization should be created, but questions were raised about its scope. I expressed my conviction that there should be a theological basis as a criterion for membership, but Oldham felt that this was not the moment to discuss the issue.

A sub-committee was established to draft a plan. S. McCrea Cavert has related how he proposed the name of the new body: "Then Archbishop Temple finally asked: 'What name shall we now give the child?' I timidly suggested: 'How about World Council of Churches?' After a brief silence, the Archbishop remarked: 'Why not? That is what we really need and want.' "[1]

The report[2] which was adopted unanimously contains the following description of the proposed World Council of Churches:

> The new organization which is proposed shall have no power to legislate for the churches or to commit them to action without their consent; but if it is to be effective, it must deserve and win the respect of the churches in such measure that the people of greatest influence in the life of the churches may be willing to give time and thought to its work.
>
> Further, the witness which the Church in the modern world is called to give is such that in certain spheres the predominant voice in the utterance of it must be that of lay people holding posts of responsibility and influence in the secular world.
>
> For both these reasons, a first-class intelligence staff is indispensable in order that material for discussion and action may be adequately prepared.

It is not difficult to recognize the hand of Dr Oldham in these paragraphs. We find again the emphasis on study and research, and on the full participation of the laity. The most important new element is the proposal that the Assembly, a fully representative body, meet every five years. By their membership in this Assembly, the churches determine the policy of the Council. A Central Council, later called the Central Committee, which was to meet annually, is a committee of the General Assembly, and carries out its policy. With regard to the composition of this Central Council or Committee, the thirty-five members proposed a system of regional representation. Thus, the representatives from North America were to be appointed through the Federal Council of Churches there; and of the United Kingdom and those of the European Continent in such a manner as the churches of these areas might decide. There would be places reserved for the Orthodox Church; the representatives of the younger churches would be appointed on the advice of the International Missionary Council and a number of places would be given to delegates from South Africa, Australasia and other areas not otherwise represented.

The choice of this method of representation was clearly influenced by the Constitution of the Universal Christian Council for Life and Work with its regional sections, and by the Constitution of the International Missionary Council with its National Christian Councils. This was to prove the weakest element in the Westfield College plan, for it made the World Council of Churches dependent on councils of churches rather than on the churches themselves.

With regard to relations with other ecumenical bodies, it was clear that the World Council would have strong links with the International Missionary Council, since the two bodies had a common interest in bringing the churches of Asia, Africa and Latin America fully in the ecumenical movement. The fact that at Westfield only six out of sixty places on the Central Council were assigned to these three continents shows that the new body had still a great deal to learn before it would really merit the name of *World* Council.

In another aspect of representation, however, the thirty-five members showed that they could look forward. Their report stated that one-third of the representatives in each case should be laymen or women so far as possible. "In the event of the number of laymen and women elected being less than one-third of the total, the Council shall allot to one or more of the appointing bodies additional places up to the number of ten to be filled by laymen or women."

The question of the relationship with the World Alliance for Promoting Friendship through the Churches was a delicate one, because it meant the end of very close association between the Alliance and Life and Work. This was regretted by many, but it was the logical consequence of the choice of a structure in which the churches would have the power to make decisions. The leaders of the World Alliance desired to maintain its unofficial character, as is shown by a statement made by William Pierson Merril, the President of the World Alliance, who attended the Westfield meeting. This statement was to the effect that the representatives of the Alliance assembled in 1937 "decided with practical unanimity on a policy that included (1) the most cordial cooperation with the World Council, and (2) the maintenance of the World Allliance as a movement based on individual loyalty, with no official relation to any religious organization."[3]

12. The world conferences at Oxford and Edinburgh, 1937

The great question now was whether the World Conference of Life and Work at Oxford and that of Faith and Order in Edinburgh would accept what seemed to many a very daring proposal.

In Oxford, the proposal was referred to meetings of the regional sections, which provided the opportunity for full discussion. William Adams Brown, chairman of the meeting of delegates from the United States of America, succeeded in gaining the support of those who were at first hesitant or even opposed to the plan. Marc Boegner, the chairman of the meeting of delegates from the European continent, also reported unanimous acceptance and, when the final vote was taken in the plenary meeting, there were only two dissenting voices.

Clearly there was a general conviction that the plan was the logical outcome of recent trends in the ecumenical movement. It had now found expression in the conclusions of the Oxford conference. The message of the conference, drafted by William Temple, said: "The first duty of the Church, and its greatest service to the world, is that it be in very deed the Church — confessing the true faith, committed to the fulfilment of the will of Christ, its only Lord, and united in him in a fellowship of love and service." The conference was keenly aware of the Church's responsibility in a secularized and paganized world and so, as the Committee of Thirty-Five had put it, was anxious "to facilitate the more effective action of the Christian Church in the modern world" and wished to create a world council of churches for this purpose.

The World Conference on Faith and Order dealt with the plan for a world council in a different way. In his sermon at the opening service, Archbishop Temple, chairman of the conference, made a strong statement on the subject. Referring to the conference at Oxford, he said: "It has approved a method whereby, if we are also led to approve it, the *Una Sancta* will be provided with a more permanent and more effectual means of declaring itself and its judgment than at any time for four hundred, perhaps for eight hundred years." The conference decided to appoint a special committee of sixty members, under the chairmanship of Dr J. Ross Stevenson. This committee had before it the report of the Committee of Thirty-Five, together with the explanatory notes on it prepared by Archbishop Temple,[1] in which he described the plan as providing "the ecumenical movement as a whole with a more effective means of self-expression". He went on to say that "if the new organization were to win the confidence of the churches, it would do something to provide a voice for non-Roman Christendom", and added that "it seemed to be a step towards the *koinonia ton ekklesion* which the Ecumenical Patriarch long ago expressed a desire to see".

Stevenson's committee presented a unanimous report. It proposed that the conference should give a sympathetic welcome to the general plan without committing itself to details and should commend it to the favourable consideration of the churches. The report recommended, however, that the continuation committee of the conference should be instructed to approve the completed plan only if a number of guarantees were incorporated. Some of these were proposed to ensure that, in the realm of Faith and Order, the same principles would be observed as had characterized the movement from the start. Thus, the "Basis" of the Faith and Order movement ("Christian bodies which accept our Lord Jesus Christ as God and Saviour") should continue to be the basis on which invitations to conferences on Faith and Order would be issued and the conferences themselves conducted. Other guarantees related to the ecclesiastical character of the new council, stipulating that it should consist of official representatives of the churches. These guarantees created the impression that the Edinburgh conference was to some degree suspicious of the new development. On 26 April 1938, Oldham wrote to me that "the Faith and Order movement intends to be married and with equal determination to remain single". In fact, however, these conditions could be met without difficulty, and this enabled the commission to arrive at a unanimous report. As Stevenson put it, these recommendations helped "meet the misgivings which some had about the proposal and provide their remedy".

Temple spoke strongly in favour of the commission report and propsed the following additional safeguard: "Any council formed before the first meeting of the assembly shall be called provisional, and the assembly, representing all the churches, shall have complete freedom to determine the constitution of the central council."

There followed a short debate when some questions were asked, but nobody expressed disagreement with the recommendations. Some members asked that they should be voted on immediately. Others proposed that the debate should be adjourned. The second group was defeated. When the vote on the report was taken there was only one against.

The council plan was discussed again when the section on "The Church's Unity in Life and Worship" presented its report. The last part of this report dealt with steps to be taken in order to move forward towards unity, and had been prepared by a sub-section chaired by John R. Mott. The final step was formulated in the following way:

> We approve the proposal submitted to the Edinburgh and Oxford conferences that the Life and Work and Faith and Order movements be united to form a World Council of Churches. The plan should conserve the distinctive character and values of both movements. To this end it is essential that, while freedom should be exercised in the formation of special committees, the churches as such should come together on the basis of the doctrine of the incarnation. The largest success of the plan depends upon efficient representative national bodies, as these will ensure adequate representation of every communion.[2]

John R. Mott in an introductory speech on the report commended the proposal for a World Council of Churches. In the discussion that followed, the Rt Rev. A.C. Headlam, Bishop of Gloucester, recorded his opposition to the proposal; for, "if such a council were to exist, and if it passed resolutions on public affairs, it might do a very considerable amount of harm".[3] He believed that many members of the conference were opposed to any definite connection with Life and Work.

Bishop Headlam's impression concerning the opposition of a number of members was based on the situation as it was before Stevenson's committee had begun its work. He had in mind the critical attitude of several Anglican delegates. But the Anglicans had as many as 13 representatives among the sixty members of the committee. In the course of the discussion their fears were allayed by the explanations given and by the conditions which were formulated and so the committee could produce a unanimous report. It was specially important that Bishop Craig Stewart of the Episcopal Church of the USA, who had at first taken a critical attitude, had now become an active supporter of the world council plan. He was later chosen to serve as one of the seven representatives of Faith and Order in the committee which was empowered to draft the constitution for the World Council.[4]

In this first debate about the World Council, Bishop Headlam was the only speaker who spoke against the World Council plan.

On 16 August, a revised draft report was presented to the conference. The first sentence of the paragraph on the World Council of Churches now read: "If the churches adopt the proposal to form a World Council of Churches which has been approved in principle by this conference as well as by the world conference held at Oxford, we think it should be so designed as to conserve the distinctive character and value of each of the movements represented in the two conferences."[5]

In the discussion of the draft, the Bishop of Gloucester moved the addition of the words: "Some members of the conference desire to record their opposition to the formation of such a council", and made it clear that, if these words were not added, he would vote against the report, even though, according to standing orders, the report could be adopted only *remine contradicente*. The chairman asked for evidence that there were "some" who disagreed, and one delegate ranged himself on the side of the Bishop of Gloucester. The first two sentences of the draft were therefore amended as follows: "This conference as well as the world conference held at Oxford have approved in principle the proposal that the churches should form a council of churches. Some members of this conference desire to place on record their opposition to this proposal, but we are agreed that if the churches should adopt it, the council should be so designed as to conserve the distinctive character and value of each of the movements represented in the two conferences."[6]

The Bishop of Gloucester's antipathy towards the Life and Work movement was well-known, for he had made no secret of the fact that he disapproved of the position that movement, and in particular its spokesman, the Bishop of Chichester, had taken with regard to the church conflict in Germany. As late as June 1937, Bishop Headlam had stated publicly that National Socialism was not anti-

Christian, and that the Third Reich was based upon positive orthodox Christianity.[7] It was not however then known to what extent Bishop Headlam had collaborated with Bishop Heckel, the head of the Department of Foreign Office (*Aussenamt*) of the German Evangelical Church, who had close relations with the Foreign Office of the Third Reich. Later, on the basis of documents from the archives of the Aussenamt, Armin Boyens, in his book *Kirchenkampf und Ökumene 1933-1939,*[8] described Heckel's strong reaction against the formation of the World Council. In National Socialist circles, Life and Work was considered a dangerous organization, while Faith and Order enjoyed a better reputation. From Heckel's point of view, therefore, it would be a disastrous mistake to unite the two movements. He had therefore sent a special emissary who first saw the Bishop of Gloucester with instructions to inform him that "if the World Council is carried through then there will be a first-rate crisis".

This emissary from Heckel managed to get himself appointed as an interpreter at the Edinburgh conference and there presented Heckel's point of view to Archbishop Temple. In order to avoid an open breach with the official German Evangelical Church, Temple and Oldham went so far as to agree to the somewhat irregular step of permitting Heckel to substitute himself for Bishop Marahrens of Hanover at the first session of the Committee of Fourteen appointed (as will be related in the following chapter) at Oxford and Edinburgh to bring the World Council into being. Although he did not make any trouble at that meeting, Heckel clearly shared the hope of the Bishop of Gloucester that the Faith and Order movement could be saved from an alliance with Life and Work.

There were now very few opponents to the Council plan. Many of those who had hesitated were ready to support it because trusted leaders like William Temple, John R. Mott, William Adams Brown, George Bell, Germanos of Thyateira and Marc Boegner had approved it. Thus, at the last debate on the subject, John R. Mott answered another negative speech by the Bishop of Gloucester in this way: "First, the sub-section and the whole of Section IV approved it (the formation of the Council). It is not surprising since this last practical step is an enabling of all the previous sixteen. It is the keystone of the arch we have been seeking to build here."[9] William Adams Brown explained his support of the plan by saying: "It is the one thing we have got that will appeal to the imagination of the people, that the ordinary layman and woman will understand."[10]

13. The World Council's constitution drafted at Utrecht, 1938

The Committee of Fourteen was formed through the appointment of seven members each by the two world conferences and it was given the task of forming the World Council. This Committee decided at its first meeing that, in order to gain the full cooperation of the churches, it would be necessary to call together a representative group of church leaders to assist in the drawing up of a constitution. The meeting of the Committee of Fourteen with the church leaders took place in Utrecht in May 1938, with Archbishop Temple in the chair and Dr Oldham as secretary. The plan elaborated at Westfield College was used as a starting point, and three problems were discussed in greater detail: the authority of the Council, its doctrinal basis, and the way in which representatives to the Assembly and the Central Committee should be chosen.

The question of the Council's authority had been treated very briefly in the report of the Committee of Thirty-five. There it had been stated that the World Council of Churches would have no power to legislate for the churches, or to commit them to action without their consent. Despite this asssurance, the question had arisen as to whether the new Council would not, in fact, become a centralized ecclesiastical body, acting independently. The most violent reaction came from the spokesmen for National Socialist ideology, influenced by Alfred Rosenberg's declaration in his book *Protestantische Rompilger* ("Protestant Pilgrims to Rome"), that the ecumenical movement was simply a bad imitation of the example set by Rome, a view which he saw as confirmed by the formation of the World Council. There was also, however, a good deal of anxiety among other church leaders about the danger of setting up a "superchurch".

At Utrecht, there was general agreement that the Council could not commit the churches to action without their consent. Bishop Perry of the Episcopal Church in the United States of America said: "The fear is that a small body would come to exercise executive power without being representative of the churches. But if the churches knew that the assembly would provide ways of contact and witness it would reassure them.... The churches must be protected against the domination of a small body having powers only rightly exercised by the churches themselves as representative bodies." The meeting agreed on the following wording for the article in the constitution concerning authority:

> The World Council shall offer counsel and provide opportunity for united action in matters of common interest. It may take action on behalf of constituent churches in such matters as one or more of them may commit to it. It shall have authority to call regional and world conferences on specific subjects as occasion may require. The World Council shall not legislate for the churches; nor shall it act for them in any manner except as indicated above or as may hereafter be specified by the constituent churches.[1]

In the explanatory memorandum sent to the churches together with the proposed constitution, Archbishop Temple made this comment: "It (the World Council) is not a federation as commonly understood, and its Assembly and Central Committee will have no constitutional authority whatever over its constituent churches. Any authority that it may have will consist in the weight which it carries with the churches by its own wisdom."

The question of the doctrinal basis led to a long discussion. Faith and Order had, from the beginning, issued its invitations to churches "which accept our Lord Jesus Christ as God and Saviour", and made it clear that it would continue to use this basis. Life and Work had had no fixed basis. It had first, therefore, to be decided if the Council should establish a doctrinal basis, and if so, what form this should take.

Some arguments against a definite basis were heard at the meeting. Letters were read from the Association for Liberal Christianity, from the Unitarian Church in Britain and the Czechoslovak Church, expressing the fear that the adoption of a basis such as that of Faith and Order would alienate liberal churches from the ecumenical movement. This point of view was, however, defended at the meeting by only one speaker. All the others agreed that a doctrinal basis was necessary. There was some discussion of the possibility of using the Nicene or the Apostles' Creed for the purpose. Most speakers however expressed a preference for the adoption of the basis used by Faith and Order, on which so many churches had met together since 1910, particularly as Faith and Order desired to continue to use it for its own conferences. The wish was, however, also expressed by a number of delegates that it should be left to each church to decide for itself whether it could join a council having this as its basis.

William Temple summarized the outcome of the discussion in the explanatory memorandum:

> It (the Council) stands on faith in our Lord Jesus Christ as God and Saviour. As its brevity shows, the basis is an affirmation of the Christian faith of the participating churches, and not a credal test to judge churches or persons. It is an affirmation of the Incarnation and the Atonement. The Council desires to be a fellowship of those churches which accept these truths. But it does not concern itself with the manner in which the churches interpret them. It will therefore be the responsibility of each particular church to decide whether it can collaborate on this basis.[2]

The matter of representation was not discussed as fully as it should have been. It has been seen that, except for the Orthodox churches, the plan made at Westfield College had foreseen representation mainly on the regional principle. The Lutheran World Convention and the Baptist World Alliance had, however, in the meantime, expressed a strong preference for representation on confessional lines. At Utrecht, Dr Knubel of the United Lutheran Church of America expressed regret that the proposals made by the Lutherans and the Baptists had been ignored. The Lutherans at the meeting were prepared, though with regret, to accept the proposed method, but claimed the right to discuss the matter further with the Committee of Fourteen. A regional plan was then adopted, that is that a certain number of places in the Assembly and the Central Committee would be assigned to each region, and the member churches in these regions would allocate these places "in such a manner as they may decide". As the question had not been sufficiently studied and discussed, this could not be considered the last word on the subject. It would arise again on a future occasion.

There was strong support for the Westfield proposals concerning the representation of laymen and women. The proposed constitution therefore contained this provision: "In order to secure that approximately one-third of the Assembly shall consist of lay persons, the Central Committee, in consultation with the different areas and groups, shall suggest plans to achieve this end", and, in allocating places on the Central Committee to different areas, it was specified how many of these places should be filled by lay persons — for example, for the continent of Europe, there should be five lay persons in a delegation of twenty-two, for the United States of America, five among eighteen, and so on.

With regard to interim arrangements, it was decided immediately to set up a Provisional Committee for the World Council (in Process of Formation), composed of the members of the Committee of Fourteen and their alternates, together with a few members appointed by the administrative committee of Life and Work and the continuation committee of Faith and Order. Life and Work had not appointed a continuation committee at Oxford, and so decided to ask the Provisional Committee to take over its task. Faith and Order desired to retain its independence until the process of formation of the World Council was completed.

The Provisional Committee then chose the following officers: Chairman: Archbishop Temple; Vice-chairmen: Pastor Marc Boegner, Archbishop Germanos and Dr John R. Mott; General Secretary: Dr W.A. Visser 't Hooft; Associate General Secretaries: Dr William Paton and Dr Henry Smith Leiper.

14. The last hurdle: Faith and Order approves

At the Edinburgh Conference in 1937, Faith and Order had made its final approval of the completed plan conditional to the incorporation of a number of guarantees and, at the meeting of its continuation committee in Clarens in 1938, it was further discussed as to whether the constitution worked out at Utrecht fulfilled the desires expressed in Edinburgh.

The chairman of the Clarens meeting, Archbishop Temple, in reviewing its work recommended that the requirements of the delegates at Edinburgh be printed in full in the text of the constitution. As to whether there was a danger that Faith and Order would be side-tracked in its tasks by Life and Work, the Archbishop said that he had been told that Life and Work greatly feared that it might be absorbed by Faith and Order.

Professor Hartford of the Church of Ireland moved then that the Edinburgh demand that, in matters of common interest to all the churches and pertaining to Faith and Order, the Council should always proceed in accordance with the basis on which the Lausanne and Edinburgh conferences had been called and conducted, should be inserted into the text of the constitution. To the further question as to whether the word "basis" in this connection meant only the theological basis, or the fundamental principles of Faith and Order, it was suggested that the wider interpretation was correct. The motion was carried *nemine contradicente*. A second motion that would have obliged the Council to carry out every recommendation of the Faith and Order Commission was defeated.

When Pastor Boegner asked for a unanimous vote to indicate that the Committee believed the Edinburgh requirements had been sufficiently secured, the Bishop of Gloucester stated that, though he regretted disturbing the unanimity of the committee, he belived that this proposal would mean the end of the Faith and Order movement as it had functioned previously. Working independently, the movement had made steady progress, but association with Life and Work would inevitably involve it in political questions, and these would adversely affect the fulfilment of its task. The Bishop therefore announced his intention of voting against the motion.

Pastor Boegner's motion was put to the vote, and carried with two dissentient voices. Canon Hodgson then reported that, in the postal vote which had been taken, 83 members had expressed the opinion that the constitution satisfied the Edinburgh requirements, and only two had voted in the negative.

The greatest hurdle had thus been crossed. It was a blessing that, in this difficult period from Westfield College to Clarens, the discussions had been guided by that incomparable chairman, Archbishop Temple, who combined the necessary patience with firmness, and whose leadership was accepted by all.

After the meeting, the Bishop of Gloucester reported to that other strong opponent of the World Council, Bishop Heckel of Berlin: "As you may have expected, we were not successful in preventing the World Council, but considerable efforts were made to take care that in its constitution the rights of Faith and Order were preserved. I know many people have misgivings about the whole thing, but the people who have engineered it have been much too clever for us."[1]

15. The invitations are sent out

The Committee of Fourteen was now able to send out the invitation to churches to take part in the establishment of the World Council of Churches. In October and November 1938, the hundred and ninety-six churches which had been invited to the Oxford and Edinburgh conferences each received four documents: a letter of invitation signed by the members of the Committee of Fourteen, the draft constitution, an explanatory memorandum on it drawn up by Archbishop Temple,[1] and a memorandum on the interim arrangements made for the period until the process of formation was completed.

The letter of invitation explained the deeper motivation of the proposal. It read:

> We forward this invitation to take part in the establishment of a World Council of Churches, at a time of critical importance. The whole Christian Church finds itself face to face with problems, needs, and forces which constitute a challenge to its principles and even a menace to its life. Often before in its long history the Church has found in such a challenge the occasion for exhibiting afresh to the world its character and unity.

> The proposal now made to establish a consultative body representing all the churches which accept its basis and approve its aims, and to which each should bring its own distinctive witness, arises by the inevitable process from the development of various movements since 1910 — and especially of those movements commonly called Life and Work and Faith and Order. But it comes before us at a moment when the need for a presentation of the unity of Christian people in the face of un-Christian and anti-Christian tendencies in the world is of peculiar importance. We hope that it may be considered in relation to the special tasks of the worldwide Church in the world today.

Yet it is not only or chiefly because it may be of practical convenience and utility that we commend this scheme. Rather it is because the very nature of the Church demands that it shall make manifest to the world the unity in Christ of all who believe in him. The full unity of the Church is something for which we must still work and pray. But there exists a unity in allegiance to our Lord for the manifestation of which we are responsible. We may not pretend that the existing unity among Christians is greater than in fact it is; but we should act upon it so far as it is already a reality. We can do this both by frank discussion of our differences on the basis of our common allegiance, which is the task of the Faith and Order Movement, and by combining to think out our witness in the face of the needs of the world, which is the task of the Life and Work Movement. But much may be gained by drawing these together, for already the two Movements have been led, by the logic of their own principles, to occupy the same ground. And both will gain by seeing these special problems against the background of the Church's primary task of world evangelization.[2]

The letter carried the signature of the following: M.E. Aubrey (Baptist Union of Great Britain and Ireland), G.F. Barbour (Church of Scotland), Marc Boegner (Reformed Church of France), William Adams Brown (Presbyterian Church in the USA), George Cicestr (George Bell, Church of England), H. Fuglsang-Damgaard (Church of Denmark), William Ebor (William Temple, Church of England), Erling Eidem (Church of Sweden), G. Florovsky (Russian Orthodox Church), Germanos, Archbishop of Thyateira (Ecumenical Patriarchate), John R. Mott (Methodist Episcopal Church, USA), S.F.H.J. Berkelbach van der Sprenkel (Netherlands Reformed Church), J. Ross Stevenson (Presbyterian Church in the USA), and George Craig Stewart (Protestant Episcopal Church in the USA).

Archbishop Temple also sent a personal letter to the Cardinal Secretary of State of the Roman Catholic Church, stating that he had understood from previous communications that the Church of Rome would not desire to be formally associated with the Council, but courtesy required that the Holy See be informed of what was proposed, and suggesting that an exchange of information and unofficial consultation might still be possible. The reply received indicated that there was no obstacle to confidential consultation with English Roman Catholic bishops or the Apostolic Delegate, or to the exchange of confidential information and opinion with Roman Catholic theologians.

16. The International Missionary Council offers to help

At the time when the plans for the World Council were under way, the International Missionary Council was not willing to give up its independence and become a part of it. The Missionary Council had in its constituency a number of missionary societies which did not want to come under the control of the churches. There was also the concern that the churches of Europe and North America might dominate the new Council to such an extent that the younger churches from other continents would not have the place they deserved. It was also not yet clear whether assistance to the churches in their task of mission and evangelism would be among the principal functions of the World Council.

On the other hand, there were pressing reasons for close cooperation between the new World Council and the International Missionary Council. The purpose of the missionary movement was the founding of churches and, as Oldham had already predicted in 1920, at some stage in its development the International Missionary Council would have to make way for a council of churches. It was further to be expected that the younger churches, when they became fully autonomous and able to take their full place in the ecumenical movement, would want to be associated not only with missionary bodies in the West, but also with their sister churches. Finally, there were extremely close personal links between the two organizations. Oldham had been a central figure in both; John R. Mott, who was chairman of the IMC, had played a leading role at Oxford and Edinburgh and was vice-chairman of the provisional committee of the World Council, and the provisional committee had decided at Utrecht to request the IMC for the part-time service of William Paton as one of its associate general secretaries.

A few months later, when the IMC held its World Missionary Conference at Tambaram, Madras, more than half of the delegates represented churches in Asia, Africa and Latin America. It was clear that the younger churches were eager to participate in the ecumenical movement.

William Paton advocated close relations between the IMC and the WCC; he said that the latter symbolized "the existence of a universal fellowship of Christians really living and active in spite of our ecclesiastical divisions", while the IMC stood for the evangelization of the world and had therefore something of priceless value to bring into the whole Christian ecumenical movement. The IMC conference at Tambaram expressed its interest in the plan for the World Council of Churches but decided that the distinctive service and organization of the IMC should be maintained.

Two other concrete decisions were taken at Tambaram which had great significance for the World Council. The first was the decision to respond positively to the provisional committee's request for the part-time service of William Paton as Associate General Secretary. With his worldwide contacts, his wisdom and his energy, Paton rendered invaluable services in the critical years of the Council's formation.

The second decision was that the IMC and the WCC should form a joint committee to make proposals for collaboration. This suggestion was accepted by the World Council's provisional committee, and it was decided that the joint committee should be under the chairmanship of Mott, with Paton as its secretary. In spite of his great age, Mott gave vigorous leadership to this body, which facilitated the entry into the World Council of the younger churches, and also made a survey of common tasks and responsibilites. It further set in motion a process of reflection on the common calling of the two Councils, which was to lead to the "association" between them, decided upon in 1948 and to their integration, decided upon in 1961.

17. The war years and the first post-war meeting

When the provisional committee was formed, it was hoped that the process of formation would be completed in three years. At its meeting in St Germain in 1939, August 1941 was chosen as the date for the first assembly. As it turned out, because of World War II and its aftermath, the period of formation and provisional existence lasted for ten years.

Would this fragile body survive? Would not the war lead to an ecumenical moratorium? In my report to the first post-war meeting of the provisional committee in Geneva in February 1946, I said:

> The war came. And at first it seemed as if it would at least mean that the clock of ecumenical history would be definitely set back. The staff became smaller and smaller. Many plans had to be cancelled. And it appeared for a time as if it would be impossible to maintain interchurch relationships. But right in the midst of war the tide turned. New contacts between the churches lost in frequency, they gained in intensity and depth. The war years did not weaken the Council. On the contrary, they became the occasion to demonstrate how inevitable its existence is if the Church is to live up to its calling. Never before in ecumenical history had it become so very clear that there are urgent tasks which no church alone can perform and that there must be a body, however small and weak, which by its very existence demonstrates the ultimate cohesion of the churches. For those who have had the privilege to be intimately associated with the Council in wartime, these years will always stand out as the time when the ecumenical task was spiritually easy and simple, because in spite of the enormous technical difficulties, the marching orders were so very clear and the basic unity of the defenders of the faith was so deeply felt.[1]

In an address at the ecumenical service in the Cathedral of St Pierre, in Geneva, on the same occasion, Bishop Berggrav said:

I wondered what it would mean to meet Christians from all over the world. My surprise is that it is no surprise. It was self-evident because in these last years we have lived more intimately with each other than in times when we could communicate with each other. We prayed together more, we listened together more to the Word of God, our hearts were together more. This is only the manifestation of what we knew already, that today God has not a weak world Church, but one founded by himself. The time is past when the worldwide fellowship of Christians was only an experiment full of hesitation. During the war Christ has said to us: "My Christians, you are one".[2]

The war years strengthened the determination of the churches to manifest their fellowship. This is shown most clearly by the fact that, in this period of crisis and uncertainty, so many churches decided to participate in the establishment of the World Council. At the first meeting after the war, it was reported that ninety had already accepted the invitation, and thus expressed their confidence in the future of the Council.

Another impressive demonstration of the desire to overcome all barriers to fellowship between the churches was the meeting held at Stuttgart in October 1945 of leaders of the German Evangelical Church and representatives of the World Council. It was here that the well-known "Stuttgart Declaration" was made. In this Declaration, the German churchmen clearly expressed that they were conscious of their implication in the guilt of the German people, their determination to make a new beginning and their desire to participate fully in the ecumenical fellowship. The World Council delegation, and later a number of churches, responded with humility and deep appreciation to this truly Christian declaration, which contributed significantly to create the right atmosphere for the final preparations of the First Assembly of the World Council.

During the war it became clear that the World Council would have to fulfill a wider range of functions than had been envisaged at the outset. We have seen that the authors of the original plan had placed strong emphasis on study, and already there were in existence the study commissions of Faith and Order on doctrinal issues, and the groups of Life and Work which, under Oldham's leadership, were striving to find a solution to the problems created by the emerging trends in modern society. Another function for the Council had been stressed by Söderblom and Temple, that of giving a common voice to the churches, to enable them to render a more effective witness. Not much thought had, however, been given to practical tasks in the realms of mutual service and solidarity. Dr Adolf Keller was indeed directing the European Central Office for Inter-church Aid, but this had not had the support it deserved. Now the tremendous needs which faced the churches as a result of the war obliged the Council to undertake several practical tasks, including aid to refugees, the chaplaincy service to prisoners of war, and the distribution of the holy scriptures. In 1942, Dr S. McCrea Cavert of the Federal Council of Churches in the United States of America succeeded in reaching Geneva and he and I together made plans for an ecumenical approach to the enormous task of reconstructing church life in Europe and helping the needy.

It was clear that a Council which considered itself to be a *koinonia* or fellowship in the New Testament sense of the word had to practise solidarity, and it was remembered that the Life and Work conference at Stockholm had used the slogan "Communio in Adorando et in Serviendo".

Both Faith and Order and Life and Work had tried to associate the younger generation with their work. At the World Christian Youth Conference in Amsterdam, held a few weeks before the outbreak of war, young people from all parts of the world had responded most eagerly to the vision of a world Christian community. The provisional committee therefore decided soon after the end of the war to accept a share in the responsibility for a second world conference of Christian youth, to be held in Oslo in 1947. It was also decided to set up an Ecumenical Institute at the Château de Bossey, near Geneva, to train leaders who would carry the ecumenical spirit into the life of the churches and of society.

Finally, there was an urgent need for a continuous and thoroughly competent service to the churches in the field of international affairs. In this matter, the World Council and the International Missionary Council decided to cooperate and it was agreed that a Commission of the Churches on International Affairs should be established. With the active help of the Commission on Just and Durable Peace, a committee in the United States, a conference was prepared to work out the programme of the CCIA. This was held in Cambridge in 1946.

That such a considerable programme should be undertaken by a committee which had only a provisional character was of course most unsatisfactory. It was therefore decided that, in spite of all the difficulties of the post-war situation, the first Assembly of the World Council should be held in 1948.

18. Second thoughts on representation and membership

In the Westfield College plan and in the draft constitution prepared at Utrecht, the representation of the churches in the Council had been based on the regional principle, though an exception was made for the Orthodox churches. But this regional approach was criticized by the advocates of the confessional principle. Thus eight Lutheran churches in the United States of America proposed in 1945 to amend the constitution so as to provide for Lutheran representation both in the Assembly and in the Central Committee on a confessional basis. These and other critics of the original plan felt that a structure based on world confessional families would be able to deal more directly with the confessional differences which had led to separation. They felt that the confessional point of view was far more important for churches than the territorial one. The defenders of the regional principle pointed out that the confessional approach would tend to freeze confessional positions and make advance towards unity in national situations even more difficult.

Discussion led to an agreement that, in the matter of representation, both the regional and the confessional factors would be taken into consideration. For some, this represented a compromise, but many others welcomed it as a deliberate choice for a World Council in which the member churches would be the basic units. Exclusive emphasis on the regional principle would have tended gradually to make the World Council a council of national or regional councils. Exclusive emphasis on the confessional principle, on the other hand, would have made the World Council a council of confessional families or communions. Both these were undesirable because the confessional and the national or regional bodies were essentially consultative and had no authority over their member churches. For the World Council, itself a body without canonical authority, it was essential to be in direct touch with the churches which were competent to speak officially in World Council meetings on behalf of their members and to translate World Council proposals into concrete action.

The provisional committee decided therefore at its meeting in Buckhill Falls (USA) in 1947 to propose to the first Assembly an amendment with regard to the representation of the churches in the Assembly and the Central Committee. According to this amendment, which was adopted by the Assembly, the seats in the Assembly were to be allocated by the Central Committee, and the membership of the Central Committee was to be distributed among the member churches by the Assembly. In both cases, due regard was to be given to such factors as numerical importance, adequate confessional representation and adequate geographical distribution. This formula had also the advantage that regional and confessional aspects of representation would both be taken into account. It meant, however, that the allocation of seats in the Assembly and of places on the Central Committee would be difficult, and would demand much wisdom and good will on the part of all concerned.

Another amendment adopted by the Assembly provided that world confessional associations and national councils of churches, to be designated by the Central Committee, might be invited to send to the Assembly representatives who would have the status of consultants.

In 1947, the policy as to requirements for membership was more precisely defined. The principal requirement was, of course, agreement with the Basis upon which the Council had been formed, but four other criteria were established. The first was autonomy, that is to say that a church is responsible to no other church for the conduct of its own life. The second was stability and the third was size, while the fourth was the relationship to other churches. It was also decided that, before churches which were members of confessional world organizations were admitted, the advice of these organizations would be sought.

ΕΓΚΥΚΛΙΟΣ ΣΥΝΟΔΙΚΗ

ΤΗΣ ΕΚΚΛΗΣΙΑΣ ΚΩΝΣΤΑΝΤΙΝΟΥΠΟΛΕΩΣ

ΠΡΟΣ ΤΑΣ

ΑΠΑΝΤΑΧΟΥ ΕΚΚΛΗΣΙΑΣ ΤΟΥ ΧΡΙΣΤΟΥ

ENCYCLIQUE

DE L'EGLISE DE CONSTANTINOPLE

A TOUTES

LES EGLISES DU MONDE

ΕΚ ΤΟΥ ΠΑΤΡΙΑΡΧΙΚΟΥ ΤΥΠΟΓΡΑΦΕΙΟΥ

1920

INTERNATIONAL MISSIONARY CONFERENCE
CRANS, JUNE 22-28, 1920

Previous page: The cover of the historical 1920 Encyclical of the Ecumenical Patriarchate which launched the idea of a permanent organ of fellowship and cooperation between the churches. The Encyclical begins: "Our Church is of opinion that a closer intercourse with each other, and a mutual understanding between the several Christian churches, is not prevented by the doctrinal differences existing between them, and that such an understanding is highly desirable and necessary..." The two things that could most contribute to this were "the removal of all mutual distrust and friction between the various churches..." and the revival and strengthening of love between them (see Appendix I).

Above: Participants at the International Missionary Conference at the Château de Crans, near Geneva, in 1920 at which Dr Oldham made his prediction concerning a "world league of churches". J. H. Oldham is sixth from the left in the front row, and John R. Mott is second on his left.

Right: The members of the Continuation Committee set up by the conference on Life and Work in Stockholm in 1925. Archbishop Söderblom is second from the right, in the front, with the Bishop of Winchester, Frank Theodore Woods, to his right, and Archbishop Germanos of Thyateira, Exarch of the Ecumenical Patriarchate, behind them. At the back (arrowed) is George Bell, Dean of Canterbury (later Bishop of Chichester), and to his immediate left is Prof. William Adams Brown of Union Theological Seminary, New York.

The Stockholm conference brought together many of the people who were to play a crucial role in events leading up to the creation of the World Council of Churches. Above: left, Archbishop Germanos; second from left, Patriarch Photios of Alexandria; fourth from left, Archbishop Söderblom. Below, left to right: George Bell, Dean of Canterbury; Crown Prince Gustav Adolf of Sweden; Archbishop Söderblom; and Frank Theodore Woods, Bishop of Winchester.

The plan for a World Council of Churches received substantial support at the world conference on Faith and Order in Edinburgh, 1937. The report stated: "This conference, as well as the world conference held at Oxford, have approved in principle the proposal that the churches should form a council of churches." Archbishop Germanos, with conference chairman Archbishop William Temple of York, and Church of Scotland Moderator Dugald Macfarlane.

In 1938 at Utrecht the Committee of Fourteen met with church leaders to draw up a constitution for the proposed World Council and choose a provisional committee. Front row, right to left: Archbishop Germanos, Dr Ross Stevenson (USA), Pastor Marc Boegner (France), Dr William Adams Brown (USA), Dr John R. Mott (USA), Archbishop Temple, Bishop Irenaios (Yugoslavia), and Dr Visser 't Hooft.

Twenty-nine years after advocating the idea of a league of churches, Archbishop Germanos (right) had the satisfaction of being present at the First Assembly of the World Council of Churches, in Amsterdam, 1948. With him at the presidents' table are (from left to right) Archbishop Eidem (Sweden), Pastor Boegner (immediately behind the archbishop), Dr Visser 't Hooft, Archbishop Fisher of Canterbury and Dr John R. Mott.

The first Executive Committee of the World Council came together at the Château de Bossey, near Geneva, in 1949. Left to right: T. C. Luke (Sierra Leone), Pastor Boegner (President of the French Protestant Federation), Archbishop Germanos, and Dr Visser 't Hooft.

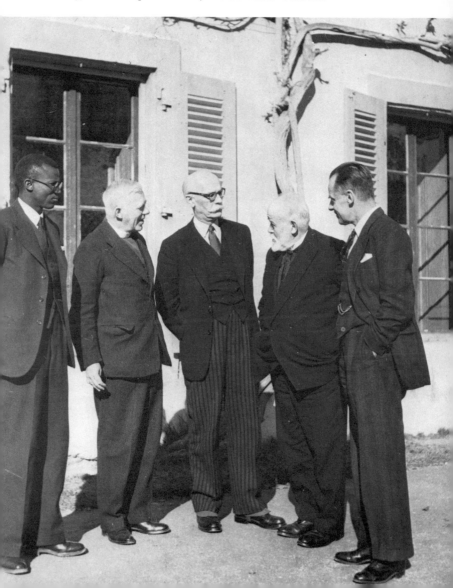

The Central Committee at Toronto in 1950 adopted what became known as the Toronto Statement, which was an attempt to describe the Council's understanding of its identity and role (see Appendix V). From left to right: Prof. Baillie (Scotland), Archbishop Germanos, Dr Mott, Pastor Boegner, Bishop Bell, Dr Martin Niemöller (Germany), Dr Visser 't Hooft and Dr Sisco (Canada).

19. The first Assembly: Amsterdam 1948

A large international conference can produce substantial results within the short period of twelve days only if it is very thoroughly prepared. The preparation for the first Assembly in 1948 started only in 1946, and the task was difficult. Once again, Dr S. McCrea Cavert, general secretary of the Federal Council of Churches in the United States, contributed greatly as chairman of the committee of arrangements. The main theme, "Man's Disorder and God's Design", was considered in four parts, by four sections of the meeting. The Faith and Order subject was "The Universal Church in God's Design", while that of Life and Work was "The Church and the Disorder of Society". The interest of the newly created Commission of the Churches on International Affairs was reflected in the section dealing with "The Church and the International Disorder"; the perspective of the International Missionary Council, and of the Secretariat for Evangelism which the World Council hoped to set up, in the discussion of "The Church's Witness to God's Design". By this process of decentralization, it was possible to produce the preparatory material in time. Coordination was ensured by the Study Department Commission of which Prof. Henry van Dusen of Union Theological Seminary was chairman.

The Assembly met on 22 August 1948. Delegates came from 147 churches and 44 countries, ready to participate in the establishment of the World Council. All confessional families except the Roman Catholics were represented. A number of Roman Catholics had been invited to attend as observers, but they could not accept the invitation because in June the Holy Office had issued a *Monitum* to the effect that no Roman Catholic would receive permission to attend.

The Orthodox churches of the four ancient Patriarchates of Alexandria, Antioch, Constantinople and Jerusalem, the Church of Greece and the Orthodox Church in the United States of America, and the Russian Exarchate in Western Europe were represented. Other Orthodox churches however followed the guidance given at a consultation held in Moscow just before the Assembly. There, the favourable reports on the ecumenical movement made by theologians from Bulgaria and Romania were overshadowed by others which misrepresented the motives of those planning to form the World Council. These churches therefore decided to refrain from participation in the World Council "in its present form".[1]

The younger churches were more strongly represented than they had been at Oxford and Edinburgh; they were mainly Asian churches, which sent 22 delegates. Very few young churches of Africa and Latin America were as yet ready to join the Council.

The pioneer generation was represented by John R. Mott, who had presided over the Edinburgh Conference of 1910, and J.H. Oldham, whose prediction, made in 1920, had at last come true. Archbishop Germanos was present, and saw before his eyes the realization of the vision which he had in 1919, while Prof. Hamilcar Alivisatos of Athens could remember how he had outlined the plan for a world council in Geneva in 1920. Bishop Brilioth, for his part, was surely thinking of the initiative taken in 1919 by his father-in-law, Archbishop Söderblom, with whom he had worked closely.

The constitution drafted at Utrecht, with the amendments proposed by the provisional committee, was adopted without difficulty. It was agreed that the Basis set forth in the constitution was adequate for the current purposes of the Council, and that churches desiring changes in it should communicate these to the Central Committee for study, and for presentation to the second Assembly. Meanwhile, the Central Committee was to continue its study of possible changes within the Christological principle set forth in the Basis in its existing form.

The proposal of the Joint Committee of the World Council and the International Missionary Council that their association should be reflected in their titles was accepted unanimously. It was also agreed that among the functions of the World Council should be included the role of supporting the churches "in their task of evangelism".

The nominations committee under the chairmanship of Bishop Brilioth had the formidable task of applying for the first time the constitutional provisions concerning representation in the Central Committee. The committee reported:

> The Committee on Nominations in drawing up this list has had to take into consideration the numerical size of the member churches, as well as the need of adequate confessional representation and geographical distribution. Moreover, it has had to pay attention to personal qualifications and to the strongly felt desire for a fair proportion of lay men and women. It has been restricted in its choice of delegates only, and has had to be responsive to the wishes expressed by the representatives of the churches.[2]

The Chairman made this additional comment:

> We have received from the sub-committee on Women and on the Laity a request that there should be adequate representation of laity, including women, in the Central Committee. I need hardly say that we have tried hard to act in accordance with this request — also before we received it — but the limitations imposed on us through the composition of the delegations and the express wishes of the churches have not made it possible in such a degree as we should have wished.[3]

The nominations committee had also to deal with the question of the presidency of the World Council. Already in 1946 in Geneva, the provisional committee had expressed its preference for a presidium with a number of presidents, as the main groups of confessions and churches could, in this way, have their due share of leadership. Bishop Brilioth made the further point that "even if we could designate in our midst one man, as perhaps we could, whom we all trust and admire for his ability and his unfailing judgment so as to make him the one president, I fear that outside our own circle, in the churches at large, there might arise a feeling that some one church or confession would have too great a preponderance in the Council".[4]

The nominations committee therefore nominated one honorary president, in the person of John R. Mott, and six presidents. It stated in its report: "It is not possible for this committee to bind its successors, but we would go on record now as urging strongly that in future nominations and elections no church or ecclesiastical office should be entitled as of right to representation in the presidency in preference to others." This was a very important statement from a committee of outstanding leaders of the main confessions. Archbishop Söderblom had more than once expressed the opinion that there were in Christendom a number of ecclesiastical offices of such unique importance that they should have permanent seats in the highest leadership of the Council. After a closer study of the problem, however, the nominations committee had concluded that the automatic selection of these offices would create more problems that it would solve, and this was accepted by the Assembly.

Of vital importance was what the Assembly had to say on the nature of the World Council. In the report which I presented on behalf of the provisional committee at the start of the Assembly meeting, I attempted to define the significance of the Council in the following way:

> Now that the Council actually comes into existence our first task is to make it clear to ourselves and to the world what our coming together does and does not mean. The *functions* of the Council should therefore be defined as clearly as possible. The very fact that we are building a wholly new type of interchurch fellowship, for which there are no precedents in church history, means that our plans are easily misunderstood. One tenacious misunderstanding is that this Council seeks to become a super-church, a centre of ecclesiastical power, which will seek to control the churches adhering to it. Our constitution makes it as clear as possible that the Council has no such intention and claims no such authority. Moreover anyone who has worked in the ecumenical field knows that the slightest attempt to exercise such control is bound to meet with determined resistance from our churches which share the same strong sense of independence. It will, however, be useful to state again in the most unequivocal manner possible what the provisional committee has already declared in 1947, namely, that we repudiate the notion of the Council becoming a centralized administrative authority.
>
> A second misunderstanding in some quarters is that the Council pursues political ends. We live in a world obsessed by politics and large masses of men cannot believe that any great undertaking of an international character should be free from a political bias. Our task is to prove in word and deed that we serve a Lord whose realm certainly includes politics but whose saving purpose cuts across all political alignments and embraces men of *all* parties, *all* lands.
>
> What then is the true function of our Council? Our name gives us the clue to an answer. We are a council of churches, not *the* Council of the one undivided Church. Our name indicates our weakness and our shame before God, for there can be and there *is* finally only one Church of Christ on earth. Our plurality is a deep anomaly. But our name indicates also that we are aware of that situation, that we do not accept it passively, that we would move forward towards the manifestation of the One Holy Church. Our Council represents therefore an emergency solution — a stage on the road — a body living between the time of complete isolation

of the churches from each other and the time — on earth or in heaven — when it will be visibly true that there is one Shepherd and one flock.

The functions of the Council follow from this situation. We are a fellowship in which the churches after a long period of ignoring each other come to know each other. We are a fellowship in which the churches enter into serious and dynamic conversation with each other about their differences in faith, in message, in order. We are a fellowship in which Christian solidarity is practised, so that the churches aid their weak or needy sister churches. We are a fellowship in which common witness is rendered to the Lordship of Christ, in all matters on which a common word for the churches and for the world is given to us. We are above all a fellowship which seeks to express that unity in Christ already given to us and to prepare the way for a much fuller and much deeper expression of that unity.

We must not overstate our case. The very real and deep divergences between us, which will also appear in this Assembly, the absence of a great part of Christendom, are reasons for humility. But neither must we underestimate God's gift to us. If we receive what we hope to receive — namely this *koinonia* of acquaintance, of conversation, of mutual aid, of witness and of the search for full unity — then we have reason to be astonished at the goodness of God, who allows us this new beginning in our mutual relations after the long years of estrangement.[5]

In the busy days which followed, with the overloaded programme, there was not time to have a thorough discussion of these questions. Further, I do not believe that the majority of the delegates, who were newcomers to the ecumenical movement, were ready for such a discussion. One could not, therefore, expect the Assembly to contribute greatly in clarifying further the nature of the Council. However, a number of statements were made in this connection.

The constitution defined the Council as a fellowship of churches. In a message, which received wide circulation, this further description was given: "In seeking him (Christ) we find one another. Here at Amsterdam we have committed ourselves afresh to him and have covenanted with one another in constituting the World Council of Churches."

These words show that the delegates interpreted the creation of the World Council not merely in practical organizational terms. It was more than a useful administrative arrangement; it had a spiritual dimension. On the other hand, it was agreed that the Council should not overstate its own significance. Its *raison d'être* was to manifest that unity which already existed between its member churches, but, since that unity was incomplete and contradicted by discord, the Council should in no way claim to speak or act with that authority which could have been shown by a fully united church.

These two aspects of the Council's nature were also expressed in a statement first adopted by the provisional committee in Buckhill Falls in 1947, and then by the Assembly in a revised form as part of the committee report on the policy of the World Council:

> The World Council of Churches is composed of churches which acknowledge Jesus Christ as God and Saviour. They find their unity in him. They have not to create their unity; it is the gift of God. But they know that it is their duty to make common cause in the search for the expression of that unity in work and in life. The Council desires to serve the churches, which are its constituent members, as an instrument whereby they may bear witness together to their common allegiance to Jesus Christ, and cooperate in matters requiring united action. But the Council is far from desiring to usurp any of the functions which already belong to its constituent churches, or to control them, or to legislate for them, and indeed is prevented by its constitution from doing so. Moreover, while earnestly seeking fellowship in thought and action for all its members, the Council disavows any thought of becoming a single unified church structure independent of the churches which have joined in constituting the Council, or a structure dominated by a centralized administrative authority.
>
> The purpose of the Council is to express its unity in another way. Unity arises out of the love of God in Jesus Christ, which, binding the constituent churches to him, binds them to one another. It is the earnest desire of the Council that the churches may be bound closer to Christ and therefore closer to one another. In the bond of his love, they will desire continually to pray for one another and to strengthen one another, in worship and in witness, bearing one another's burdens and so fulfilling the law of Christ.[6]

The same report had this to say about public pronouncements:

> With respect to public pronouncements, the Council regards it as an essential part of its responsibility to address its own constituent members as occasion may arise, on matters which might require united attention in the realm of thought or action. Further, important issues may arise which radically affect the church and society. While it is certainly undesirable that the Council should issue such pronouncements often, and on many subjects, there will certainly be a clear obligation for the Council to speak out when vital issues concerning all churches and the whole world are at stake. But such statements will have no authority save that which they

carry by their own truth and wisdom. They will not be binding on any church unless that church has confirmed them, and made them its own.

Thus in 1948 it was stated very clearly that the World Council was not a church above the churches. It was also stated that the coming together of the churches in the World Council was connected to their calling to be the Church of Jesus Christ. It had not been made clear, however, how this understanding of the spiritual side of the nature of the Council related to the self-understanding of member churches.

20. The Church, the churches and the World Council of Churches, Toronto, 1950

From a constitutional point of view, the process of formation of the World Council was completed when the first Assembly had done its work. If, however, the word "formation" is interpreted in a more substantial way, then it must be admitted that the period of formation lasted for a further two years. It was not until 1950, at a meeting of the Central Committee held in Toronto, that the discussion of the nature of the Council and its relationship to its member churches led to the adoption of an explicit agreed statement.

Some thought had already been given to this issue between the resumption of preparations after the war in 1946 and the Assembly of 1948, but in that short period of time, a sufficient number of people had not been involved in its consideration. The preparatory volume issued for the Assembly, which contained a chapter reflecting the thinking on this point, had reached delegates only shortly before the Assembly met, so that the question was not ripe for general discussion in a large meeting, even if there had been time for a thorough consideration of it in the Assembly's programme.

In 1945, I had written a paper entitled "The World Council of Churches: its nature, its limits", which was published in English[1] and in French.[2] The Committee preparing for the Assembly section on "The Universal Church in God's Design" decided that this paper should be widely circulated, for comments and criticism, and that it should be published in a revised form in the preparatory volume on the theme of the section.

My approach to the question was naturally influenced by the situation we had gone through at the time of the church conflict in Germany during the war. My starting point was, therefore, Dietrich

Bonhoeffer's question *Ist die Ökumene Kirche?*, which he had posed during the church conflict. The Church exists only where there is a clear witness to the Lordship of Christ. Did the ecumenical movement have sufficient unity to render such witness? Was the expectation justified that the Council would provide the Protestant, Anglican and Orthodox churches with a common voice? I pointed out that there had been a remarkable dualism in the history of the ecumenical movement. The world conferences of Stockholm and Lausanne, of Oxford and Edinburgh, had at times spoken of themselves as no more than instruments for preparing for the unity of the Church, while at other times they had presented themselves as the organs that were achieving that unity in a partial but nevertheless real way. This unity, I wrote, was also present in the World Council of Churches. It could not and should not think of itself as the Church Universal, and therefore phrases like "the World Church" should not be used. The Council lacked the essential *notae ecclesiae*, the "notes of the Church", and such deep differences still existed between the member churches that they were not yet the full *koinonia* or communion as described in the Acts of the Apostles or the Epistles of St Paul. On the other hand, the World Council represented more than a merely utilitarian relationship between the churches, for when churches meet as churches, they are bound to seek to fulfill together the calling of the Church which is to proclaim the Gospel. The World Council was thus a way in which the churches sought to live together when they no longer regarded one another as strangers but were not yet able to achieve full unity. Archbishop William Temple had spoken of the World Council as a means and a method whereby the *Una Sancta* could declare itself. The World Council should not claim to be the Church Universal, but it was a body in and through which, when it pleased God, the Church Universal would find its manifestation. It did not claim any authority, but should hope that, through it, words would be spoken which would have intrinsic authority.

There was a short section in my paper on the "implications of membership". In the 1945 version, this was rather vague, and in the version printed in the Assembly volume there were phrases which were to give rise to much debate in later years. I had been struck by a comment of the Lutheran theologian, Prof. Hermann Sasse of Erlangen,[3] who had said that it was essential to state honestly that the churches saw heresies in one another's lives, but that they recognized at the same time that in other churches there were *vestigia ecclesiae,* or traces of the true Church. The task of the World Council was to show for the first time in history that the churches had enough in common to make possible real, even if not complete, unity. In the 1948 version of my paper, therefore, I wrote that joining the Council presupposed a willingness to show together the measure of unity already granted to the churches, adding however that "this does not mean that a church entering into the Council automatically recognizes the claims of all other churches in the Council to be in the full and true sense of that word parts of the Church Universal. Such recognition is most desirable, but it is the goal, not the beginning of the ecumenical process."

I knew that in this statement I was taking a position which would not find general approval. Dr van Dusen had already said of the first version of the paper that the ecumenical situation was not one of such conflict as it suggested. He considered my approach too sceptical and too modest, feeling that emphasis should be given to the basis of common conviction and understanding which was far greater than had been imagined at the time of separation. I knew however that, for many churches, it was a *conditio sine qua non* of World Council membership to recognize clearly both the fact of our unity and the fact of our disunity.

The elder statesman, J.H. Oldham, wrote a long memorandum commenting on my paper. He agreed as a starting point that the World Council could not have ecclesiastical authority, and that only when this had been made unmistakably clear could the confidence of ecclesiastical statesmen be gained. Nevertheless he believed that the utterances of the World Council would have very great authority, first as showing the mind of leading church representatives, and second, because the Holy Spirit might, to an unlimited extent, speak and exercise influence through these utterances. Oldham however added a stern warning. The Council's action could be effective on one condition only: "That condition is that at meetings which authorize such action there are present leading representatives of the churches, who in giving their approval, have reasonable confidence that if the action in question is challenged in their respective church assemblies they can successfully defend it.... Where the representatives of the churches are not in fact the leading men, the guarantee that the action of the interdenominational body will have the backing of the different churches breaks down."[4] He added that the staff should be large enough to maintain effective contact with the leaders of the churches for, if there were not sufficient staff for this, or if they lacked the capacity to win the full confidence of church leaders, the World Council would inevitably cease to function as a council of churches and would break down.

Other comments suggested that the problem of authority was not as grave as my paper had suggested. The Bishop of Chichester recalled that the Lambeth Conference also was based on the principle of "strict adherence to purely advisory functions", but it had nevertheless considerable spiritual influence. McCrea Cavert emphasized the experience of the non-authoritarian denominations in the United States, whose assemblies had acquired great practical authority. Principal N. Micklem of Oxford pointed out that spiritual authority was not a second-rate and weak authority, but the authority of the Spirit commending itself to the minds and the conscience of Christians.

After the Assembly, the question of the significance of the Council ceased to be the affair of a few ecumenical specialists, and was taken up by the religious press in many countries.

As we have seen, discussion before the Assembly had been concentrated mainly on the question of the authority of the Council, such as whether its pronouncements would have authority and, if so, of what kind. The Assembly had to a considerable extent settled that question. The constitution stated clearly that the Council should offer counsel and provide opportunities for united action, but that it was not to legislate for the churches. The Rules and Regulations stated that the authority of the Council's statements would consist only in the weight which they carried by their own truth and wisdom, and that the publication of such statements should not be held to imply that the Council had the right to speak for the churches. The Assembly had therefore used the following formula with regard to the reports of its four sections: "Received unanimously by the Assembly and commended to the churches for their serious consideration and appropriate action."

After the Assembly, another aspect of the debate received far greater attention. This was the implication of membership of the Council. In 1948 and 1949 many articles appeared which questioned whether membership in the Council had any implications for the "self-understanding" or ecclesiological position of the churches. The question took a particularly sharp form in Greece. Only a few Orthodox churches had then joined the Council, and Orthodoxy was therefore not adequately represented at its meetings. In my report to the Central Committee in 1949, I had tried to answer their question as to whether there would be room in the Council for the specific ec- clesiological position of the Orthodox Church. I wrote:

> With regard to the fundamental ecclesiological issue, the Council can state clearly and unambiguously that it has not prejudged the question of the nature of the Church. It is definitely possible for a church which con- siders itself the true Church to enter into the Council. Nothing in the of- ficial documents contains the slightest suggestion that the Council takes its stand on an ecclesiology according to which each church is to think of itself as one of many *equally* true churches. It is precisely the originality of the ecumenical movement that it invites churches many of which are as yet unable to regard each other as branches of the same tree to enter into fraternal conversation and cooperation with each other so that they may come to know each other and, if the Lord wills, advance towards a wider manifestation of unity in him.

I added that, in this respect, the situation of the Orthodox chur- ches was not fundamentally different from that of many other chur- ches in the Council.

The time had come to give a fuller answer to this question of the meaning of membership. The first occasion for this proved to be a meeting of staff members and friends of the Council with Roman Catholic ecumenists at the Istina Centre in Paris in September 1949. In many countries, the reaction of the Roman Catholic press to the creation of the World Council had been negative, but in France and in Belgium a number of articles had appeared which showed sym- pathy and understanding. Their authors, who proved to be the *avant- garde* of Roman Catholic ecumenism, had raised interesting and stimulating questions about the nature of the Council and its attitude to the Roman Catholic Church. Since the authorities had forbidden Roman Catholics to attend the Assembly, they had no first-hand in- formation about it, and were eager to discuss the matter with representatives of the World Council. We for our part felt that we could learn from this.[5]

For obvious reasons, the meeting was held in strict confidence. To facilitate discussion, I presented the subject in the form of theses. The first six of these described "What the World Council is not", as follows:

1. The WCC is not based on one particular conception of the Church.

2. To enter the WCC does not imply that a church relativizes its own conception of the Church.

3. It is not true that membership of the WCC presupposes acceptance of the doctrine that the unity of the Church is essentially spiritual and does not necessarily require visible expression.

4. It is not true that World Council membership presupposes the acceptance of a specific doctrine concerning the form which Church unity should take.

5. The role of the World Council of Churches is not to unite the churches. That can only be done by the churches themselves.

6. It is not true that the World Council desires in any way to become a super-church.

A further six theses attempted to deal with the assumptions underlying the World Council of Churches:

1. The member churches of the WCC believe, on the basis of the New Testament, that the Church in Christ is one.

2. The member churches recognize that the membership of the Church of Christ is more inclusive than the membership of any visible church (corrected in the next version: membership of their own church body).

3. The member churches of the WCC recognize in each other *vestigia ecclesiae*, that is to say elements of the true Church.

4. The member churches of the WCC do not "unchurch" each other (this sentence was left out in the next version). This does not mean that they all (next version: "necessarily") recognize each other as true, healthy or complete churches, but they consider, at least for the time being, the question of the relationship of other churches to the *Una Sancta* as an open question.

5. The member churches of the Council are ready to render common witness through word and deed with other churches to the Lord Jesus Christ.

6. The member churches of the Council consider that conversation, cooperation and common witness of the churches must be based on the common recognition that Christ is the Divine Head of the Body.

In discussing these theses, the meeting devoted a considerable amount of time to the question of authority. The report of the meeting states that it was apparently somewhat difficult for the Roman Catholics to accept on the one hand the fact that the World Council had no authority over its member churches and to admit, on the other hand, that the World Council could issue messages to the churches and to the world, messages of which the authority could be understood only in a dialectical way. Both Father Congar and Father

Danielou stressed the importance of the concept of *vestigia ecclesiae*, pointing out that it was necessary to arrive at a dynamic conception of these elements of the true Church.

As my efforts at the Istina meeting to clarify the nature of the World Council had apparently been found useful, I considered the advisability of submitting the series of theses to the Central Committee of the World Council, so that they could be discussed, revised and adopted as a generally agreed statement of the Council's understanding of its own nature. I added to the theses some ideas which emerged from the Istina meeting, including, I believe, the formulation: "The World Council exists in order to deal in a provisional way with an abnormal situation." The paragraph on the positive consequences to be drawn from the concept of *vestigia ecclesiae* too was strengthened in the light of the remarks made on this subject by Father Congar and Father Danielou. I added two new theses, one on the solidarity of the member churches and their obligation to refrain from actions which were incompatible with fraternal relations, and another on mutual spiritual assistance for the sake of the renewal of the life of the churches. At the end of the document, I pointed out that the distinction between the conditions which had to be fulfilled so that the churches might enter into relations of conversation and cooperation in the World Council and those which had to be fulfilled to achieve full unity was fundamental. The World Council was an emergency measure and had only a provisional task.

At its meeting in Bossey, in February 1950, the Executive Committee agreed that a second version of the document should be drawn up and that, in its revised form, it should be submitted to the Central Committee at its meeting in July 1950.

The document had thus changed its character. In the first version my definitions were simply a personal contribution to the discussion and therefore bore my signature. In its second version, the document ceased to be the expression of a personal opinion and had to be put into the form of a draft statement prepared in the hope that, after revision, it would be adopted by a large committee of men and women of many nationalities and churches. In this task, I received much help from my colleagues, especially from O.S. Tomkins, at that time the secretary of Faith and Order.

At its meeting in Toronto, the Central Committee appointed a sub-committee to review and revise this document and to report back on it. While the sub-committee shortened the document considerably and rearranged the order of the theses, none was left out, except the one which stated that membership of the Council did not imply acceptance of the doctrine that the unity of the Church consisted in the unity of the invisible Church.

The presentation of the revised document to the meeting in Toronto led to a debate of considerable intensity in which very real divergences on the conception of the Council were revealed. A number of members were disturbed by the fact that the document referred, not only to the unity discovered by the churches in the Council, but also to their disunity, thus interpreting the Council as a fellowship in which members experienced tension and conflict as well as fraternal concord.

The opposition concentrated on two points. The first was the sentence in the introductory section which ran: "The World Council exists in order to deal in a provisional way with an abnormal situation, that is with division between existing churches which ought not to be, because it is in contradiction with the very nature of the Church." This was sharply criticized by van Dusen and others because it seemed to imply that the World Council had only a provisional existence; they believed that it represented a permanent necessity in the life of the churches, and felt that the view that the unity of the churches in the World Council was all the unity which the churches should demand, had not been considered seriously in the draft before the Committee.

It was agreed to make an amendment, and the final draft accepted by the Central Committee read: "The World Council deals in a provisional way with divisions between existing churches, which ought not to be, because they contradict the very nature of the Church." This left open the question as to whether all divisions, and the Council itself, should be superseded by a united Church.

The second issue was much more difficult and became the subject of heated debate in two long sessions of the Committee. It was the question of mutual recognition of the member churches. The first text presented by the sub-committee to the Central Committee stated: "IV: 4. The member churches of the World Council do not necessarily recognize each other as true, healthy or complete churches, but they consider the relationship of other churches to the *Una Sancta* as a question for mutual consideration."

This thesis became the target of strong attack. It was asked how the Council could be considered as a fellowship of churches, when some churches regarded others as untrue, unhealthy and incomplete. Other speakers believed that the true facts about relationships within the Council should not be concealed. The sub-committee was asked to revise the document again. In the new draft, the sub-committee inserted at the beginning the statement on the nature of the World Council which had been adopted by the First Assembly in 1948. The controversial thesis was rephrased as follows:

> IV:4. The member churches of the World Council consider the relationships of other churches to the Holy Catholic Church which the Creeds profess as a subject for mutual consideration. Nevertheless, membership does not imply that each church must regard the other member churches as churches in the true and full sense of the word.

However, even this somewhat less offensive formulation was still criticized by some who said that it was not the function of any church to tell other churches that they are not full and true churches. At this point, Father George Florovsky of the Russian Orthodox Church in Emigration spoke with deep feeling, making an impressive appeal to fellow committee members. The issue, he said, was not simply the formulation of some sentences in a document: much more was at stake. His church regarded the other churches as *essentially* incomplete. If, as was possible, this tradition represented a viewpoint too difficult for some, it might be time to part. In the World Council, representatives of a high doctrine of the church were in a minority, but it was better to satisfy such a minority. In response, some Lutheran, Anglican and Reformed committee members pointed out that the document merely described the situation as it then existed in the World Council, and made no claim to describe what ought to be the situation. Father Florovsky, they felt, should not be more concerned than others, as the Orthodox were not alone in taking this point of view. Dr John Baillie of Edinburgh affirmed that the World Council had been made possible only because it had included those who "unchurched" each other.

This discussion was extremely useful. There was the general feeling that it was the most important and valuable exchange of views ever heard in the committee. At a later session, a slightly revised version of the document was presented. The former title, "The Ecclesiological Significance of the World Council of Churches" became the sub-title, and the main title was now "The Church, the Churches and the World Council of Churches". This was clearly better, for it was anomalous to emphasize "ecclesiological significance" when the statement argued that the Council had no specific ecclesiological position of its own.

The revised draft was now accepted, commended for study and comment by the churches, and became known as the Toronto Statement.[6]

After the meeting I wrote in the "World Council Diary", in *The Ecumenical Review* of October 1950:

> During the course of that searching discussion, there were moments of anxiety when it seemed that the World Council had come to a real crisis in its history. But it proved to be a crisis unto life, for at the end of the discussion all present had arrived at a deeper understanding both of the very real differences which exist between the member churches of the Council in their conception of the Church and also of the no less real work of the Holy Spirit through which these churches are brought into fellowship with each other.

The discussion was continued in the religious press. In *The Ecumenical Review* of April 1951, ten reactions were published, most of them positive. Archbishop Germanos, who had published a Greek translation of the Toronto Statement, wrote that it would contribute greatly to the removal of still existing difficulties and thus help to perfect the friendship (*amphictyony*) of the churches of Christ. The Bishop of Malmesbury, of the Church of England, felt that the statement went right to the heart of the matter. The inclusion of the thesis IV:4 concerning recognition was vital if there was to be a Catholic element in the Council. The membership of the Orthodox churches was regarded as a matter of great importance by the Anglican communion, which could not give support to a purely pan-Protestant alliance. According to Prof. Peter Brunner, a Lutheran, it was a singular spiritual experience granted to the Church in our time that members of churches which were obliged to exclude one another from communion still admitted one another in love to be living members of the Body of Christ.

There were also critical voices. Van Dusen was of the opinion that the statement was too patently oriented towards those of more extreme "catholic" convictions, who looked upon the World Council with misgiving, if not with positive distrust, while Clarence T. Craig of the United States questioned how long the unstable equilibrium described in the statement could last.

Two reactions combined appreciation with an expression of concern about the future. Archbishop Brilioth thought it would be fatal if the majority of members were content that the present divisions should continue to the end. "A certain discontent, a wider vision, a more intense yearning after a fuller unity is an element which is necessary for the *bene esse*, perhaps for the *esse* of the World Council of Churches."

Bishop Newbigin of the Church of South India felt it was natural that the churches should seek assurance that, in joining the Council, they would not be compelled to abandon their own convictions about the Church. He saw a danger in being too reassuring. While clearly a provisional neutrality had to be asked of the Council on matters on which its member churches were divided, it should be made even clearer that this neutrality was provisional. The possibility had to be left open that the Council might have to abandon its neutral position on some of the ecclesiological issues which divided Christians. In other words, it had to be emphasized that the statement defined the starting point, and not the way or the goal. To commit the Council to neutrality as a permanent principle would be to reduce it to the status of a debating society.

It seemed to me at the time and it still seems to me today that Bishop Newbigin's comments are lucid and persuasive. He had perhaps underestimated the dynamic elements in the statement, for it had stressed the duty of the churches to make common cause in the search for the expression, in work and in life, of their unity in Christ. It stated that divisions contradicted the very nature of the Church and had spoken of the need for a holy dissatisfaction with the existing situation, and of the duty of each church to do its utmost for the manifestation of the Church in its oneness. Further, the statement had said that the Council existed to break the deadlock between the churches, so it was obvious that it did not seek "to petrify the *status quo*". The use of the expression "ecclesiological neutrality", which was not contained in the statement, was misleading unless it was made clear that this neutrality was limited to ecclesiologically controversial issues, and also that it was provisional. Bishop Newbigin was, however, correct in pointing out that sufficient stress had not been given to an important point, that as the churches entered into cooperation and dialogue, their aim should be to widen their area of agreement. This meant that the "ecclesiological neutrality" of the Council was not only limited, but also provisional, in the sense that it was a stage on the road to greater unity.

That the Toronto Statement was in fact not considered as a final or complete interpretation of the Council's comprehension of its own identity and role became clear in the following years. The subject was discussed again and again, and attention was called to aspects of the Council's life which had not been sufficiently defined in Toronto. Thus, in a meeting of the Central Committee held in Rolle in 1951, an important statement on "The Calling of the Church to Mission and Unity" was adopted, in which the Council was described as an organ of the ecumenical movement, concerned with the whole task of the whole Church of bringing the gospel to the whole world.

When I addressed the third World Conference on Faith and Order at Lund in 1952, I said that in Toronto we had sought to answer the question: "How can a church justify its membership in the World Council of Churches in terms of its traditional ecclesiological convictions?" I then went on to ask the next, and even more difficult question: "How can we give adequate expression to the spiritual reality which exists in the ecumenical movement?"[7]

In 1954, the preparatory commission for the Faith and Order section of the Second Assembly held that year at Evanston made the Toronto Statement the "keystone" of its survey. It reported that the statement had been much discussed in the churches and that, of the churches which had responded, hardly any had taken issue with the statement as a whole. It was, in the opinion of the commission, merely a contribution to a continuing discussion, and by no means said the last word on the nature and function of the World Council and the inter-relationship of the member churches.[8]

One of the principal themes of the Central Committee meeting at Davos in 1955 was "Various Meanings of Unity and the Unity which the World Council Seeks to Promote". In my introduction[9] I pointed out that a number of statements had been made in the reports and resolutions of the assemblies and in meetings of the Central Committee about the nature of Church unity. We had come to understand more and more the meaning of unity in Christ, and should speak as substantially about Church unity as was possible without breaking the promise made to member churches that no pressure would be put on them to adopt particular, concrete schemes to achieve this end.

Again in New Delhi in 1961, a number of steps were taken which were of importance to the Council in its efforts towards self-understanding. The Assembly accepted a revised and expanded text of the Basis, i.e. the first article of the Constitution, which now ran: "The World Council of Churches is a fellowship of churches which confess the Lord Jesus Christ as God and Saviour according to the Scriptures and therefore seek to fulfill together their common calling to the glory of the one God, Father, Son and Holy Spirit."[10] In the report on "Christian Witness, Proselytism and Religious Liberty", the implications of World Council membership for the relations between the churches were clarified and the report of the section on unity provided a new description of Church unity. It ran: "The Toronto Statement was a landmark in the World Council's thinking about itself and its relation to work for unity. Here we seek to carry that thought a stage further, not by dictating to the churches their conception of unity, but by suggesting for further study an attempt to express more clearly the nature of our common goal."[11]

So much discussion had taken place during the time of which we are speaking that it may well be asked why a revised version of the Toronto Statement was not produced, incorporating the new insights. A first attempt to do this was made by Faith and Order in 1956, but it was not felt that the new draft had by then reached a stage where it could be adopted as a revision of the Toronto Statement.

A second attempt was made at Montreal in 1963, during the fourth World Conference on Faith and Order. Some delegates proposed that a statement should be drafted which would show to what extent the World Council at that time manifested the *notae ecclesiae* of the classical creeds. Others objected strongly, particularly though not exclusively, delegates of Eastern Orthodox churches. The report of the section on "The Church in the Purpose of God" as adopted by the conference confirmed that, while the Toronto Statement had proved very helpful and remained a basic document of the Council, there had been important new developments in the Council's life since 1950. Member churches used different categories of thought to express their convictions about the Church, and so tended to arrive at different interpretations of the Council.

The following paragraph of this report is especially relevant:[12]

> The Council gratefully acknowledges that in sustained fellowship it has received something new, namely, an enrichment of our Christian existence and a new vision of our common Christian task in the world. The manifestations of this new experience are seen in several ways: a common allegiance to the one Lord; an increasing progress towards a common life

of prayer, praise and proclamation; the sharing of burdens, difficulties and pains; an increasing doctrinal consensus without compromise (for example, with regard to the meaning of baptism); intensified Bible study; the tendencies towards mutual recognition of members among some of the member churches. We do not concur in the precise description of this experience, but we are agreed that it is a new dimension in the Council. We therefore express the ardent wish that this new common experience should grow and increase steadily through God's help and guidance leading us to final unity.

When I addressed the Central Committee at Rochester, a few days after the Montreal conference, I pointed out that we were trying to define ecumenical realities in the thought-forms of the pre-ecumenical age. I concluded: "It is better to live with a reality which transcends definition than to live with a definition which claims more substance than exists in reality." Prof. Hamilcar Alivisatos, who forty-three years before in Geneva had explained the Constantinople plan to create a Council, was the first speaker in the discussion. He said that the Orthodox Church was very happy to recognize the cooperation between the churches in the Council, but could not recognize the Council as having prerogatives which belonged to the true Church. Further discussion led to the conclusion that, as Prof. Berkhof said: "We can live beyond Toronto, but we cannot formulate beyond Toronto."

These short observations about the later history of the Toronto Statement belong to the period of development rather than to that of the formation of the Council. I have included them here to show the place that Statement has taken in the history of the Council and also because its purpose has often been misunderstood. Even Bruno Chenu's penetrating study on the documents concerning the ecclesiological significance of the World Council contains a few passages which are based on a misunderstanding of the Toronto Statement. After emphasizing its importance, he summarizes his critical evaluation which suggests that it may perhaps be a diplomatic and political rather than an ecclesiological document. Further, he considers its contents as strategical and opportunist.[13] His choice of the word "diplomatic" is astonishing, for in the same paragraph he writes that the statement reflects a desire to speak openly about the tensions in the life of the Council. It should also be recalled that in the discussion at Toronto, the statement had been defended on the very ground that it did not conceal these facts,[14] and such frankness hardly deserves to be described as "diplomacy". As for the word "opportunist", this is defined in the dictionary as "seeking immediate advantage with little regard for principles or ultimate consequences". It was in no way the purpose of the Toronto Statement to seek such advantage; on the contrary, it was an attempt to define the fundamental principles of the Council and to build a strong foundation for its future development. The statement can and should be criticized, but in terms which do justice to its intent. That intent was not to produce a systematic treatise on ecclesiology in general, but to formulate as concretely as possible the ecclesiological principles which were implicit in the formation of the Council and which had to be stated explicitly to guide it in the years to come. I see no objection to calling such an intent strategic, but I prefer to think of it as the normal task of those responsible for planning policy.

In the chapter dealing with the problem in his recent book *Conflict over the Ecumenical Movement*, Ulrich Duchrow asks: "How is the World Council of Churches related to the Church of Christ?" This is useful as a reminder that, after a period in which ecclesiological questions had been neglected, the time has come to continue the interrupted debate on the subject. Duchrow's theses deserve to be taken seriously. Here as we deal with the genesis and formation of the World Council, I must, however, confine myself to a few remarks on the interpretation which Duchrow gives of the history of the Council.

With regard to the Toronto Statement, Duchrow follows Chenu in emphasizing its ecclesiological neutrality, but does not make sufficiently clear that this neutrality is limited.[15] Moreover, he does not do justice to the other ways in which the World Council has shown its understanding of its role, ways which must be considered together with the Toronto Statement. Duchrow concludes that resistance to the attribution of ecclesiological significance to the Council was in the last analysis due to the refusal of ecclesiastical institutions to allow themselves to be called into question.[16] This seems to me to be too simple an explanation of the ecumenical problem, which does not take sufficiently seriously the reality of ecclesiological convictions. Real ecumenism presupposes a respect for the beliefs of the partners with whom one enters into dialogue, treating them not as an ideological smokescreen but as real convictions. Clearly, non-theological factors play an important role in the churches' ecumenical policy, and institutional self-assertion is one of the strongest of these factors. We must however not become so obsessed with them that we neglect the very real theological convictions which also influence that policy. The World Council is the forum where those holding these convictions enter into conversation, and where no church need fear that it will be put under pressure to change its position — except the pressure that may be exercised by new truth discovered in the ecumenical encounter. The originality and the *raison d'être* of the World Council lie precisely in this respect for differences. It would be easier to form a council of churches with similar ecclesiologies, but such a council would not be able to undertake the greater task of bringing together all the Christian churches. Since 1920, when the Church of Constantinople addressed its Encyclical to *all* churches, when Söderblom fought in Geneva to make sure that *all* Christian communions should be invited to the conference of Life and Work, and when Faith and Order prepared its conference as a fully ecumenical gathering, the choice had been made for this more difficult kind of ecumenical movement, which would produce a paradoxical kind of world council in which unity and disunity would be in constant tension. Such a council has great need to hear the voice of the Confessing Church of which Duchrow seeks to remind us, but Bonhoeffer's ecclesiology cannot be made the one and only criterion for its life.

21. Conclusion

The question is sometimes asked: "Who founded the World Council? Who was its chief architect?" The story which I have tried to tell here shows that it is not possible to answer that question by giving the names of a few people. We must rather think in terms of a kind of relay race — of a few people carrying the torch for a while, and then passing it on to others.

At the very beginning we find two such torch-bearers, Metropolitan Germanos (Strinopoulos) in the south and Archbishop Nathan Söderblom in the north, who met in Geneva in 1920 and made common cause. Then, at the Stockholm conference of 1925, it was George Bell, later Bishop of Chichester, almost the only participant who spoke of the desirability of a permanent council. In the following years, Söderblom, Germanos and Bell cooperated in creating the Universal Christian Council for Life and Work. This however proved to be insufficiently rooted in the churches, so the next torch-bearer, William Adams Brown of New York, began a campaign to bring the various ecumenical bodies together in a more unified organization. He was followed by J.H. Oldham, who already in 1920 had predicted that the time would soon be ripe for the formation of a worldwide association of churches, and who was to organize the Life and Work Conference held at Oxford in 1937. He was the key figure in ecumenical development during the period in which the plan for a world council received concrete form, at the Westfield College meeting of 1937 and the Utrecht meeting of 1938. By this time, there was also another torch-bearer, Archbishop William Temple who, with his very great spiritual influence, spoke for the World Council plan in the United States of America in 1935, presided at the meetings in Westfield and Utrecht, and helped greatly to convince Faith and Order of the urgency of the new move. Another was Samuel McCrea Cavert of the Federal Council in the United States, who proposed the name "World Council of Churches".

At the world conference of 1937, and especially at the Faith and Order conference in Edinburgh, John R. Mott, with his great experience and wide vision, played a crucial role. Again, in 1938 at the World Missionary Conference in Madras, together with William Paton, Mott prepared the way for the entry into the Council of the churches of Asia, Africa and Latin America. When the Provisional Committee of the World Council of Churches (in process of formation) was formed in Utrecht in 1938, the main responsibility for making the plan known to the churches and for the formation of the Council was entrusted to a general secretariat with three offices, one in London, under William Paton, one in New York under Henry Smith Leiper and one in Geneva where I myself was responsible. That the flame was not extinguished during World War II was due largely to Pastor Marc Boegner of France and Dr Alphons Koechlin of Switzerland, who helped the staff to keep the ecumenical network in operation.

It is significant that among these torch-bearers, we find men of different confessions or denominations: Orthodox, Lutheran, Anglican, Reformed or Presbyterian, and Methodist. It cannot be said that the idea of the Council belonged to any one confession, for many made their contribution.

* * *

It is now possible to identify the main motives and convictions which gave the World Council plan its substance and form. But in attempting the task, I shall have to repeat a number of phrases, sentences and passages which have already appeared in this book. These contain a crystallization or distillation of ideas and concepts which have played an important part in the thinking and development of the Council.

First of all, the purpose of the planners was to persuade the churches to accept full responsibility for the fulfilment of the ecumenical task. The Encyclical of Constantinople was addressed "Unto the Churches of Christ Everywhere" and invited "the judgment and the opinion of the other sister churches in the East and of the venerable Christian churches in the West and everywhere in the world''. Söderblom's plan contained an enumeration of the main confessions with their ecclesiological authorities. This turning to the historic churches was not an obvious step, for up to that time almost all successful ecumenical activities had been carried out by movements independent of the churches. Further, not a few ecumenically active Christians, including many of the leaders of the World Alliance for Promoting Friendship through the Churches, believed that the future of the ecumenical movement would be endangered if it surrendered its autonomy and put itself in the hands of the official church bodies.

In a document written just before his death[1] Söderblom explained why he had turned to the churches, instead of to individuals or groups in them. He felt that the originality of the Life and Work conference at Stockholm in 1925 had consisted in the attempt made there to listen to the Church as such, and to mobilize it for the task ahead. The presence of so many ecclesiastical dignitaries at the Stockholm conference has been criticized, but if the cause of unity was to become the cause of the Church, the participation of church leaders was essential. It would have been much easier to organize a meeting exclusively of people already convinced of the ecumenical task. The Church in its institutional form is a heavy instrument, and when a large number of staunch church people meet, the light of the Gospel does not easily shine through their deliberations. Because we wished to make the cause of unity the cause of official church bodies we had not the right to choose the easier way.

In 1937 at the Westfield meeting, it was this same conviction that led to the difficult decision to bring Life and Work and Faith and Order together, even though this terminated the close relationship then existing between Life and Work and the World Alliance for Friendship through the Churches. This last was inevitable, because the World Alliance desired to remain independent of the churches. It was felt, however, by those advocating the union between Life and Work and Faith and Order, that the ecumenical movement could become a real force in the history of the Church and the world only if it accepted that it must become rooted in the life of the historical churches.

In the second place, the plan for the World Council was based on the conviction that the mandate of the ecumenical movement had two aspects which were closely related. It was an attempt to encourage the churches to cooperate in service to each other and to the world. When churches come together, however, the fact of their common relationship to the one and same Lord Jesus Christ becomes decisive, and it becomes difficult for them to continue to live their separate lives. The second aspect of the ecumenical task is therefore to attempt to give expression to their unity. The 1920 encyclical of Constantinople, which proposed a number of ecumenical activities of a more practical character, had not hesitated to describe the motivation of such cooperation in terms of the great statement in the Epistle to the Ephesians that Christians are "fellow heirs, members of the same body and partakers of the promise of God in Christ". When Archbishop Temple, in 1939, drafted the letter inviting the churches to join the World Council, he began by speaking of the great need for interchurch cooperation, but went on to say that it was not only nor chiefly because of its practical convenience that the scheme was proposed. The fundamental reason was that the very nature of the Church demanded that it should make manifest to the world the unity in Christ of all who believe in him.

Thirdly, the plan was motivated by the conviction that the unity of the Church is based on the action of the Lord Jesus Christ who gathers his people together. When in 1910 Bishop Brent and his colleagues founded the Faith and Order movement, they decided that the ecumenical encounter of the churches should have a clear point of departure and of reference. This basis was the acceptance of our Lord Jesus Christ as God and Saviour. The Life and Work movement did not have such a basis, but it was implicitly Christocentric, for the message of the Stockholm conference ran: "The nearer we draw to the Crucified, the nearer we come to one another." The Ecumenical Patriarchate had concluded the Encyclical with an expression of the hope that, by creating a "league", the churches might "grow up into him in all things which is the head, even Christ" (Eph. 4:15). It was therefore natural, when the Constitution for the World Council of Churches was drafted at Utrecht in 1938, that the basis of Faith and Order should be chosen as that of the Council.

The Toronto Statement ran: "The member churches of the Council believe that conversation, cooperation and common witness of the churches must be based on the common recognition that Christ is the divine Head of the Body."

Since it was felt that the Basis should be explicitly Trinitarian and should make mention of the Holy Scriptures, it was changed in 1961 to read:

> The World Council of Churches is a fellowship of churches which con-
> fess the Lord Jesus Christ as God and Saviour according to the Scriptures
> and therefore seek to fulfill together their common calling to the glory of
> the one God, Father, Son and Holy Spirit.

Fourthly, the plan was not considered as an end in itself or as a definitive solution to the problem of disunity, but as a method of mobilizing the churches for a common effort to pursue that goal.

The Encyclical of Constantinople had stated that the plan would be useful for the preparation and advancement of that blessed union which would be consummated in the future in accordance with the will of God. Söderblom had also had in mind an ecumenical development passing through different stages. He said: "We cannot afford to remain separated and in a state of unnecessary impotence caused by our separation, up to the time when we shall be truly united in faith and church organization."[2]

In the introductory report which I made on behalf of the provisional committee to the first Assembly of the World Council in 1948 I said: "Our Council represents therefore an emergency solution — a stage on the road — a body living between the time of complete isolation of the churches from each other and the time — on earth or in heaven — when it will be visibly true that there is one Shepherd and one flock."[3]

In the fifth place, the plan sought to provide an instrument through which the solidarity of the churches might find clear expression.

The 1920 Encyclical of the Ecumenical Patriarchate had referred to the willingness to offer aid and mutual help as one of the marks of a league of churches, and the Stockholm conference of 1925 had used as its motto: *Communio in adorando et serviendo oecumenica.* Churches entering into such a communion accepted the obligation to pray for one another and to render mutual assistance. As soon as the provisional committee for the World Council was formed, it agreed to accept responsibility for service to refugees. When World War II broke out, a chaplaincy service to prisoners of war was organized, and before long this became the largest department of the Council. Such solidarity also involved what had been underlined in the 1920 Encyclical, and declared in the Toronto Statement when it urged churches "to refrain from such actions as are incompatible with brotherly relationships". In other words, proselytism was to be avoided in interchurch relationships.

Nor is such solidarity of the churches merely "churchly" and introverted. It expresses itself also in a common concern for the suffering, the needy and the hungry of all faiths in all parts of the world. Thus the programme of interchurch aid under which responsibility for service to refugees had already been accepted, was at an early stage widened to include "world service", that is to say, assistance to victims of natural disasters or of famine and poverty.

As a sixth point, the plan provided for that mutual encouragement and exhortation which was such a prominent feature of the early Christian churches, as described in the letters of St Paul. The ecumenical significance of this paraklesis is clearly described in the message of the first Assembly of the World Council: "As we have talked with each other, we have begun to understand how our separation has prevented us from receiving correction from one another in Christ. And because we lacked this correction, the world has often heard from us not the Word of God but the words of men."

The Toronto Statement also spoke of this aspect of the ecumenical task: "The member churches enter into spiritual relationships through which they seek to learn from each other and to give help to each other in order that the Body of Christ may be built up and that the life of the churches may be renewed." In other words, the existence of the World Council provided the opportunity to set in motion once again that exchange and sharing of the *charismata*, the diverse spiritual gifts which St Paul described in the twelfth chapter of the First Epistle to the Corinthians.

Next, the plan sought to express the dimension of wholeness in the calling of the churches. The definition that the word "ecumenical" embraces "everything that relates to the whole task of the whole Church to bring the Gospel to the whole world" was first used in a statement of the World Council's Central Committee on "The Calling of the Church to Mission and Unity", issued in 1951, but the idea contained in that definition was present from the beginning. The Orthodox Encyclical of 1920 had used the word "pan-Christian", that is "embracing all Christians". Söderblom found this a helpful expression, as it could also be taken to mean concern for the fullness of the gospel. When Life and Work created a more permanent organization, it chose as its name The Universal Christian Council for Life and Work.

This universality was at first rather intention than reality, for it took many years for the ecumenical movement to achieve its worldwide character. The desire for wholeness also found expression in the concern that laymen and women should be represented in the Assembly and the Central Committee of the Council. As I stated earlier, in the first attempt to outline the structure of the Council, made at Westfield College in 1937, the Committee of Thirty-Five emphasized the desirability of forming a Central Committee in which one-third of the representatives would be laymen or women, and proposed that if the number of laymen and women would be less than one-third of the total, additional places should be allotted to be filled by them. Here also the search for wholeness proved to be a long-term task, for implementation does not depend in the first place on action by the World Council but on decisions taken by each of the member churches. The first Assembly of the Council expressed its concern for the participation of the whole Church through its committees on "The Life and Work of Women in the Church", "The Significance of the Laity in the Church" and in its youth delegation.

As an eighth and final point, the plan sought to enable the churches to render their common witness to the world. Söderblom said in a memorandum shared with the meeting in Oud Wassenaar in 1919: "A common voice must be created for the Christian conscience. I advocate an Ecumenical Council representing Christendom in a spiritual way."[4] Temple wrote in his explanatory notes on the proposed World Council, which were circulated to the delegates of the Faith and Order conference of 1937: "If the new organization were to win the confidence of the churches, it would do something to provide a voice for non-Roman Christendom."[5] The first Assembly stated in 1948 that the Council desired to serve the churches as an instrument whereby they might bear witness together of their common allegiance to Jesus Christ and cooperate in matters requiring united action.[6]

At the very beginning of the discussion on interchurch collaboration it was understood that one of the chief purposes of this cooperation was to speak with one voice to the world on the Christian approach to social and international problems. Thus the call to the Stockholm Conference on Life and Work, issued in 1924 and signed by Archbishop Söderblom, Archbishop Germanos, the Bishop of Winchester and other church leaders, states specifically that the world's greatest need was the Christian way of life, not merely in personal and social behaviour, but in public opinion and its outcome in public action.[7] The conference itself stated: "The conference has deepened and purified our devotion to the Captain of our salvation. Responding to his call 'Follow me', we have in the presence of the cross accepted the urgent duty of applying his gospel to all realms of human life — industrial, social, political and international."[8] The World Council's concern for the creation of a truly responsible society and for justice and peace in the realm of international and inter-racial relations is therefore not a product of the 1960s or 1970s, but belongs to its heritage from the period of the founders.

It must be remembered that statements of the ecumenical bodies were understood not to be binding on the Christian communions represented at their meetings unless and until they had been presented to and accepted by the authorities of each communion. In an explanatory memorandum of 1938, William Temple used the following formula: "Any authority that it (the World Council of Churches) may have will consist in the weight which it carries with the churches by its own wisdom."

* * *

The following sentences from the message of the first Assembly of the World Council of Churches in Amsterdam in 1948 interpret faithfully the significance of the genesis and formation of the Council:

> Christ has made us his own and he is not divided. In seeking him we find one another. Here at Amsterdam we have committed ourselves afresh to him, and have covenanted with one another in constituting this World Council of Churches. We intend to stay together. We call upon Christian congregations everywhere to endorse and fulfill this covenant in their relations one with another. In thankfulness to God, we commit the future to him.

Encyclical of the Ecumenical Patriarchate, 1920

"Unto the Churches of Christ everywhere"

"Love one another earnestly from the heart" (1 Pet. 1:22)

Our own church holds that rapprochement between the various Christian churches and fellowship between them is not excluded by the doctrinal differences which exist between them. In our opinion such a rapprochement is highly desirable and necessary. It would be useful in many ways for the real interest of each particular church and of the whole Christian body, and also for the preparation and advancement of that blessed union which will be completed in the future in accordance with the will of God. We therefore consider that the present time is most favourable for bringing forward this important question and studying it together.

Even if in this case, owing to antiquated prejudices, practices or pretensions, the difficulties which have so often jeopardized attempts at reunion in the past may arise or be brought up, nevertheless, in our view, since we are concerned at this initial stage only with contacts and rapprochement, these difficulties are of less importance. If there is good will and intention, they cannot and should not create an invincible and insuperable obstacle.

Wherefore, considering such an endeavour to be both possible and timely, especially in view of the hopeful establishment of the League of Nations, we venture to express below in brief our thoughts and our opinion regarding the way in which we understand this rapprochement and contact and how we consider it to be realizable; we earnestly ask and invite the judgment and the opinion of the other sister churches in the East and of the venerable Christian churches in the West and everywhere in the world.

We believe that the two following measures would greatly contribute to the rapprochement which is so much to be desired and which would be so useful, and we believe that they would be both successful and fruitful:

First, we consider as necessary and indispensable the removal and abolition of all the mutual mistrust and bitterness between the different churches which arise from the tendency of some of them to entice and proselytize adherents of other confessions. For nobody ignores what is unfortunately happening today in many places, disturbing the internal peace of the churches, especially in the East. So many troubles and sufferings are caused by other Christians and great hatred and enmity are aroused, with such insignificant results, by this tendency of some to proselytize and entice the followers of other Christian confessions.

After this essential re-establishment of sincerity and confidence between the churches, we consider,

Secondly, that above all, love should be rekindled and strengthened among the churches, so that they should no more consider one another as strangers and foreigners, but as relatives, and as being a part of the household of Christ and "fellow heirs, members of the same body and partakers of the promise of God in Christ" (Eph. 3:6).

For if the different churches are inspired by love, and place it before everything else in their judgments of others and their relationships with them, instead of increasing and widening the existing dissensions, they should be enabled to reduce and diminish them. By stirring up a right brotherly interest in the condition, the wellbeing and stability of the other churches; by readiness to take an interest in what is happening in those churches and to obtain a better knowledge of them, and by willingness to offer mutual aid and help, many good things will be achieved for the glory and the benefit both of themselves and of the Christian body. In our opinion, such a friendship and kindly disposition towards each other can be shown and demonstrated particularly in the following ways:

a) By the acceptance of a uniform calendar for the celebration of the great Christian feasts at the same time by all the churches.

b) By the exchange of brotherly letters on the occasion of the great feasts of the churches' year as is customary, and on other exceptional occasions.

c) By close relationships between the representatives of all churches wherever they may be.

d) By relationships between the theological schools and the professors of theology; by the exchange of theological and ecclesiastical reviews, and of other works published in each church.

e) By exchanging students for further training between the seminaries of the different churches.

f) By convoking pan-Christian conferences in order to examine questions of common interest to all the churches.

g) By impartial and deeper historical study of doctrinal differences both by the seminaries and in books.

h) By mutual respect for the customs and practices in different churches.

i) By allowing each other the use of chapels and cemeteries for the funerals and burials of believers of other confessions dying in foreign lands.

j) By the settlement of the question of mixed marriages between the confessions.

k) Lastly, by whole-hearted mutual assistance for the churches in their endeavours for religious advancement, charity and so on.

Such a sincere and close contact between the churches will be all the more useful and profitable for the whole body of the Church, because manifold dangers threaten not only particular churches, but all of them. These dangers attack the very foundations of the Christian faith and the essence of Christian life and society. For the terrible world war which has just finished brought to light many unhealthy symptoms in the life of the Christian peoples, and often revealed great lack of respect even for the elementary principles of justice and charity. Thus it worsened already existing wounds and opened other new ones of a more material kind, which demand the attention and care of all the churches. Alcoholism, which is increasing daily; the increase of unnecessary luxury under the pretext of bettering life and enjoying it; the voluptuousness and lust hardly covered by the cloak of freedom and emancipation of the flesh; the prevailing unchecked licentiousness and indecency in literature, painting, the theatre, and in music, under the respectable name of the development of good taste and cultivation of fine art; the deification of wealth and the contempt of higher ideals; all these and the like, as they threaten the very essence of Christian societies, are also timely topics requiring and indeed necessitating common study and cooperation by the Christian churches.

Finally, it is the duty of the churches which bear the sacred name of Christ not to forget or neglect any longer his new and great commandment of love. Nor should they continue to fall piteously behind the political authorities, who, truly applying the spirit of the Gospel and the teaching of Christ, have under happy auspices already set up the so-called League of Nations in order to defend justice and cultivate charity and agreement between the nations.

For all these reasons, being ourselves convinced of the necessity for establishing a contact and league (fellowship) between the churches and believing that the other churches share our conviction as stated above, at least as a beginning we request each one of them to send us in reply a statement of its own judgment and opinion on this matter so that, common agreement or resolution having been reached, we may proceed together to its realization, and thus "speaking the truth in love, may grow up into him in all things, which is the head, even Christ; from whom the whole body fitly joined together and compacted by that which every joint supplieth, according to the effectual working in the measure of every part, maketh increase of the body unto the edifying of itself in love" (Eph. 4:15-16).

In the Patriarchate of Constantinople
in the month of January
in the year of grace 1920

Appendix II

Archbishop Söderblom's article on "The Church and international goodwill"*

The nearest universal task of the Church may be formulated as follows: *The unity of nations must become religion or part of our religion.* The uniting element among nations is already religion. In the service of the Church we are regularly reminded of the coming of universal peace through right and justice. We hear the angelic message of peace on earth. And in these times millions of souls have clung to this thought of a community of mankind in justice as to a plank of safety on a sea of despair. Such a hope, and that alone, has for innumerable human beings been the means of saving their faith in the future, and in a justification, an ultimate purpose, behind the ghastly confusion of the world. Now the supernatural code of justice is being warped by weakness and passion, and by the power of Mammon. But however the thought may be obscure it can never die. If the unity of nations, the League of Nations, is ever to be more than a dreadful caricature or an empty form, effective only by means of might and oppression, it must become Christian in earnest, even as the very thought of it is regarded with faith and enthusiasm by hundreds of thousands who rarely if ever enter any church. Disregarding all minor differences of creed, Christianity must, as far as it is inspired by the spirit of Christ, unite in common prayer, teaching, exhortation and effort towards the strengthening of brotherhood and unity among nations.

Has the Church no need to be reminded of the Gospel of Christ? The brotherhood of mankind and the equal rights of peoples should be drawn from the Gospel itself. The ideal will remain vague, and

---

*Extracts from *The Contemporary Review*, Volume CXVI, July-December, 1919.

without prospect of realization, if it be not supported in its faith by recognition of God's fatherly care, and the conviction of Christian charity that divine mercy exists, and that God's will manifests itself throughout mankind. Neither the false pathos of an arid, bureaucratic state religion, trusting ultimately to unaided human power, nor the self-satisfied egoism of piety in restricted circles can alone avail, whether the unit concerned be small or the most magnificent clerical institution ever seen.

In all countries there are to be found some who realize that the only remedy for all this misery is Christian charity — those who have themselves experienced something of the secret of atonement and redemption, and are thus in their hearts no longer arrogant but penitent. They seek with God's aid the highest of all powers whether in great things or small, the power to forgive. Such Christians as these, in all classes and countries, should unite in prayer and in work to make the unity of nations something more than at best a lofty dream or a bold political thought — to make of it a faith able to accomplish miracles.

In social respects also the task of reformation and reconstruction necessitates working in common to maintain Christian principles. The Conference at Uppsala in 1917 also put forward proposals in this respect for a common Christian programme. This social task of the Church, however, though also of international character, may likewise be passed over here.

In order to fulfill its mission of uniting the peoples together the Church must first of all bring about the unity of its own various sections. And this unity must also find expression in an organization which can provide a common channel of utterance for Christianity generally. How can the catholicity of the Church be realized? Rome answers: I have everything in order. Leave your various spiritual homes, your chapels and churches and cathedrals. Pull them down if you will, for the sake of unity, and come over to me. Here is everything needful in the greatest hierarchical organization ever known throughout the history of religion. Is catholicity to be realized thus in the form of the Roman institution? Church history, as well as the Christian conscience in the great majority of Christians, answers as clearly as possible: No. Those parts of Christendom which have tasted spiritual freedom can never barter it away even to obtain so great a boon as outward institutional unity. And this I say with all appreciation and respect for many of our brethren and sisterhood in the Church of Rome, and for much of Roman Catholic piety.

History confirms this refusal. The anti-Reformation movement and subsequent similar attempts, especially in Austria, show what can be accomplished by force against a religious manifestation. But after the Thirty Years' War the respective values of Roman and Evangelical Christianity have remained, on the whole, constant. It is evident that two such spiritual powers must in many respects overlap — that each will appeal to temperaments seeking a new spiritual home in place of worldly interests. But even in Bavaria, for instance, where the birth-rate is higher among Catholics, the proportions remain unchanged. Even such a movement as the "Los-von-Rom", in Austria and Bohemia, which, as shown by a man like Peter Rosegger, and by the feeling in wide circles of the highest Austrian culture, is not merely political, but religious — even such a movement has achieved no essential change beyond securing some 20,000 converts. We should here rather consider the results which are being achieved by Evangelical Christianity in the United States, where out of thirty million Irish, with their descendants, scarcely more than 10 per cent are reckoned as Roman Catholics, while the percentage in Ireland itself is no less than eighty. I would here refer to an article by Peter Coudon in the Catholic Encyclopaedia, and to the calculations by the French national economist Charles Gide on the basis of the religious statistics of the United States in 1910. In any case no one can study carefully the history of the Church and the conditions of the time without being compelled to realize that the Roman Catholic programme for unity has no great prospects.

There remains, then, an evangelical catholicity, one that should allow the various religious communities to retain their creeds and organizations undisturbed, and continue their accustomed manner of divine service, but at the same time serve and strengthen the cause of spiritual unity, realizing that each one of the different sections of Christianity has its own gift of grace in the common heritage of faith, its contribution to worship, to the ideal of life and the future. An evangelical catholicity is imperative, or division will end in helpless weakness. Unity could be manifested also in externals to a certain degree owing to our unity in Christ around his cross, without waiting for the uniformity of creed and Church government.

If we look at the development of the Church, the apparent confusion of its manifold branches falls into order before our eyes. From time to time God has sent prophets into the world, but not all his people have followed them: some of the religions and churches have remained where they were before. Religious organization has not been inspired as a whole by the new spirit; instead of this, a part has isolated itself from the rest, and continued its own life, perhaps also finding new positive ideals.

Thus it was at the coming of our Saviour. The Church called itself the True Israel. But in the eyes of the Jewish congregation this was presumptuous beyond all bounds. Can any deny that Jesus was the true continuation and fulfilment, not only of Moses and the prophets, but also of the deep piety of late Judaism? Heroes of religion have also appeared without involuntarily causing disruption. St Augustine and Augustinism did, no doubt, point in some degree a new road for the Western Church, which the Oriental would not follow. But St Bernard, St Francis and others accomplished religious revivals without schism. Martin Luther is the greatest example since the introduction of Christianity of a prophet seeking, albeit vainly, to leaven the whole organism of the religious community. A new break then occurred, and was further emphasized when Rome itself gained new positive religious ideals from Ignatius Loyola.

Something of the same thrilling drama may be found in the origin of Methodism, for it was surely that "strictness of religion" which in 1729 united the brothers Wesley with two spiritual equals that gave embodiment to the new movement. But its soul was derived from Martin Luther's experience in faith, when Wesley, on his journey to America in 1735, became acquainted with it through the Herrnhuter, and later, in 1738, with the writings of Luther himself. John Wesley had likewise no desire to divide the Church against itself. But the division came after all.

When we consider these things, we find stronger grounds for an evangelical catholicity. It is the only way to avoid disintegration. A common organization must be formed of such a character as to be capable of worthily representing Christendom, without sectarian exclusion of any part. It is a magnificent and lofty task to work for greater uniformity in creed and church government, as the Conference of Faith and Order seeks to do, but the unity must find expression now among the various parts at present composing the whole.

The Catholic Church has three main divisions: the Orthodox Catholic, the Roman Catholic and the Evangelical Catholic. Among the last-named, the Lutherans amount to sixty million, Anglicans and Episcopalians to forty-five million. Methodism, which has become the most characteristic form of religion in the New World — Luther's evangelical certainty of faith, translated into soul-sufficing intensity and Anglo-Saxon capability of action — counts twenty-five million, etc. There are, of course, among these many who are only Christians in name, and many who would not even care to be called Christians. But a characteristic religious tradition has nevertheless set its mark upon their spiritual life, where any such exists. Auguste Comte, the founder of Positivism, denied the existence of God, but was nevertheless as genuine a Roman Catholic as the philosopher Immanuel Kant was a Protestant.

All this Christendom calls for a common channel of utterance. From the throne of St Peter, as well as from other parts of the Christian world, words have again and again gone forth which find echo in every truly Christian heart, and are spoken on its behalf. But a common platform is lacking. What I propose is an ecumenical council representing the whole of Christendom, and so constructed that it can speak on behalf of Christendom, guiding, warning, strengthening, praying in the common religious, moral and social matters of mankind. It should be composed partly by the appointment of men specially qualified, partly by election on broad democratic lines. It is too much to hope that Rome, with its exclusive sectarian isolation, should as yet be willing to be represented in any such common council.* There remain, then, two ancient offices in the Christian Church which should qualify their holders without question for the ecumenical council — to wit, the Patriarchate of Constantinople and the Archbishopric of Canterbury. Good reasons could be given for beginning with Evangelical Catholicism alone, in order not to complicate the actual task with the venerable orthodox part of Catholic Christendom. But there are certainly also hearty sympathies for the wider scope. The remaining parts of the Evangelical-Catholic Church in America and Europe should then be represented, according to their importance and characteristic influence, by three or four elected members. The first to be considered here would be the largest con-

---

*Bishops Anderson, Vincen and Weller of the American Episcopal Church have been on a visit to Rome and the Near East in connection with the the proposed World Conference on the Faith and Order of the Church. Pope Benedict made the deputation the traditional answer that "the unity of the Church can only occur by all returning to the Catholic Church." — *The Challenge.* "The effect of Rome's refusal is bound to quicken greatly another tendency in the Episcopal Church — that in the direction of union with Protestants." — *The Christian Century* (Boston).

tingents of evangelical catholicism, which are found in Germany and the United States. After these, the Scandinavian countries, Finland and the Baltic provinces, and further, Hungary, Switzerland, Holland and France, where Protestantism possesses a spiritual and moral influence out of proportion to the number of individuals actually to be reckoned, etc. Comprehensive international Christian organizations might also be represented, such as the Continuation Committee for Missions, the YMCA, the Student Christian Movement, the Salvation Army, etc. This ecumenical council should not be invested with any external authority, but should have and gain its influence according to the degree in which it was able to act as a spiritual power. It should speak, not *ex cathedra*, but from the depths of the Christian conscience. In appointing members a method of election based on the broadest foundation should be employed, and due regard should be taken to the historical traditions of the various religious communities, as also to their forms of constitution. In a general representative body of this character, standing for the Church as a whole, no quantitative power whatever can fill the place of the qualitative religious force which must be its sole justification. A few years back this idea was still but a dream, a new Utopia. Now the world is become far smaller, man and mankind likewise, but God is grown greater, and the Gospel and Christ also greater. The time has come, then, when we may venture to believe in the unity of Christianity, and take definite measures to express the same.

Report of the Committee of Thirty-five (Westfield College, London)

As a result of the deliberations which then took place the Committee of Thirty-five unanimously recommended that each of the two world conferences at Oxford and Edinburgh should adopt the following proposals:

1. That the conference regards it as desirable that, with a view of facilitating the more effective action of the Christian Church in the modern world, the movements known as Life and Work and Faith and Order should be more closely related in a body representative of the churches and caring for the interests of each movement.

2. That the conference approves generally the following memorandum:

> The new organization which is proposed shall have no power to legislate for the churches or to commit them to action without their consent; but if it is to be effective, it must deserve and win the respect of the churches in such measure that the people of greatest influence in the life of the churches may be willing to give time and thought to its work.
>
> Further, the witness which the Church in the modern world is called to give is such that in certain spheres the predominant voice in the utterance of it must be that of lay people holding posts of responsibility and influence in the secular world.
>
> For both these reasons, a first-class Intelligence Staff is indispensable in order that material for discussion and action may be adequately prepared.

There are certain oecumenical movements, such as the IMC, the World Alliance for International Friendship through the Churches, the WSCF, the YMCA, the YWCA, and the Central Bureau for Inter-Church Aid, with which the new body should enter into relationship both in order that the life in them may flow into the churches, and that those movements may derive stability and true perspective from the churches. The actual approach to these would need to be determined with regard to the basis and function of each.

We regard as part of the responsibility of the new body:
— to carry on the work of the two world conferences;
— to facilitate corporate action by the churches;
— to promote cooperation in study;
— to promote the growth of ecumenical consciousness in the churches;
— to consider the establishment of an ecumenical journal;
— to consider the establishment of communication with denominational federations of worldwide scope as well as with the movements named in the preceding paragraph;
— to call world conferences on specific subjects as occasion requires.

3. That the conference approves the establishment of a World Council of Churches functioning through the following bodies:
— a general assembly of representatives of the churches (in accordance with a plan to be determined later) of approximately 200 members meeting every five years;
— a central council of (approximately) 60 members which shall be the Committee of the general assembly when constituted,* meeting annually, e.g. twelve from North America appointed through the Federal Council; nine from Great Britain appointed in such manner as the churches of Great Britain may decide; eighteen from the countries on the continent of Europe (to be assigned to the different countries); nine representing the Orthodox churches; six representing the younger churches (to be appointed on the advice of the IMC); six representing South Africa, Australasia, and areas not otherwise represented (one third of the representatives in each case to be laymen or women so far as possible; in the event of the number of laymen and women elected being less than one-third of the total, the council shall allot to one or more of the appointing bodies additional places up to the number of ten to be filled by laymen or women);
— a commission for the further study of Faith and Order subjects to be appointed at Edinburgh and vacancies to be filled by the central council;

---

*The constitution for the general assembly shall be worked out by the central council in consultation with the churches and the national Christian organizations.

— a commission for the further study of Life and Work subjects to be appointed by the central council with a view to facilitating common Christian action.

4. That power be given to the central council to call into such relationship with itself as may seem good, other ecumenical movements.

5. That pending the creation of any new organization, each movement shall carry on its own activities through its own staff.

6. That the conference appoint a constituent committee of seven members to cooperate with a similar committee appointed at Edinburgh (or Oxford) to complete the details and to bring the scheme into existence.

N.B. It is suggested that the general assembly should approve the scheme for the central council, but should invite the constituents as described in section 3 to appoint the members of that council in accordance with the scheme.

Appendix IV
Explanatory memorandum on the Constitution of the World Council of Churches
by Archbishop William Temple

I. Historical

The project of a World Council of Churches has arisen out of the natural development of the two movements known as the Life and Work and Faith and Order movements. This development had led to considerable overlapping with consequent waste of time and energy. Consequently at their separate sessions held in August and September 1936, in successive weeks, the Universal Christian Council for Life and Work, and the Continuation Committee of the World Conference on Faith and Order, passed resolutions recommending the appointment of a committee to review the work of ecumenical cooperation since the Stockholm and Lausanne conferences, and to report to the Oxford and Edinburgh conferences regarding the future of the ecumenical movement.

It was further agreed that this committee should be appointed by a group representing various ecumenical movements, and should consist mainly of persons holding positions of ecclesiastical responsibility in the different churches, but should also contain representatives of the viewpoint of laymen, women and youth, and some officers of the ecumenical movements.

The group designated for this purpose, after consultation with the leaders of the movements and of the churches, constituted the Committee, known as the Committee of Thirty-Five. This Committee of Thirty-Five met at Westfield College, Hampstead, London, in July 1937, and unanimously recommended that each of the two world conferences at Oxford and Edinburgh should adopt certain proposals for the foundation of a World Council of Churches, the first of which was:

> That the conference regards it as desirable that, with a view to facilitating the more effective action of the Christian Church in the modern world, the movements known as Life and Work and Faith and Order should be more closely related in a body representative of the churches and caring for the interests of each movement.

At both world conferences the proposal was approved in principle, and each appointed seven members, with alternates, to form together a constituent committee entrusted with the duty of revising and completing the scheme, of submitting it to the churches, and of convening the World Council. The Faith and Order conference added a demand that certain guarantees for the continuity of its own work should be added, and instructed its seven representatives to cooperate in submitting the scheme to the churches only if its continuation committee had approved the scheme as incorporating the guarantees required.

The constituent Committee of Fourteen was unwilling to attempt unaided the whole discharge of its responsibility. It therefore invited the churches to appoint representatives to a conference which was held at Utrecht, 9-13 May 1938. The scheme which was prepared with the help of this conference was considered by the Faith and Order Continuation Committee which met at Clarens, from 29 August-1 September 1938. After requiring two slight modifications, it was able to resolve: "That the Constitution of the World Council as presented and amended conforms to the requirements made at Edinburgh, and the Faith and Order members of the constituent Committee of Fourteen are therefore at liberty to cooperate with their colleagues in submitting this scheme to the churches."

Two points will be noticed in this recital of the history of the proposal: first, the originators of the scheme are the governing bodies of the Faith and Order and the Life and Work movements. The World Council represents a new form of cooperation between these two movements; it will mainly be concerned to carry on their work; it is therefore to be regarded as a continuation of their activities. Secondly, at two stages the leaders of those movements called into consultation representatives of the churches, first a selected group at Westfield College in 1937, and later a strong body of officially appointed delegates at Utrecht in 1938. The scheme now submitted is that which was approved at Utrecht, modified as required by the Faith and Order Continuation Committee.

II. The Constitution

1. *The Basis*: This contains two points. First, the Council is envisaged as a fellowship of churches exercising its functions through different organs (see 5 and 6 below). It is not a federation as commonly understood, and its Assembly and Central Committee will have no constitutional authority whatever over its constituent churches. Any authority that it may have will consist in the weight which it carries with the churches by its own wisdom.

Secondly, it stands on faith in our Lord Jesus Christ as God and Saviour. As its brevity shows, the basis is an affirmation of the Christian faith of the participating churches, and not a credal test to judge churches or persons. It is an affirmation of the Incarnation and the Atonement. The Council desires to be a fellowship of those churches which accept these truths. But it does not concern itself with the manner in which the churches interpret them. It will therefore be the responsibility of each particular church to decide whether it can collaborate on this basis.

2. *Membership*: This clause calls for little comment. The second paragraph aims at securing due representation of those minority churches for which this might not be secured under any inelastic system, while avoiding any such excessive representation of very small bodies as would destroy a reasonable balance.

3. *Functions*: Here the main point of importance is that the Council exists to serve the churches, not to control them (see 4 below), and that continuance of the Faith and Order and of the Life and Work movements is put in the forefront.

4. *Authority*: This partly expands 3 above. Special attention is called to the last clause. Not only has the Council no power to legislate for the participating churches; it is also forbidden to act in their name except so far as all or any of them have commissioned it to do so.

5. *Organization*: (i) The principal authority in the council will be the *Assembly*. This will consist of representatives of the churches, directly appointed by them. It is intended to invite every church which was invited to the Oxford and Edinburgh conferences to be represented, and also others in accordance with the most careful survey which it is possible to make. Thus the continuity with the two

ecumenical movements will be preserved without exclusion of any entitled to membership.

The phrase "groups of churches" is intended to cover the case of some very small denominations and also that of churches such as some in Asia and Africa which are accustomed to act together in such matters.

In view of the nature of the Assembly's interests, great importance is attached to the securing of a considerable representation of the laity.

(ii) The *Central Committee* is to be chosen from among the members of the Assembly. The scheme provides that its members also shall be directly nominated for this service by their own churches. This will involve that in each regional group the churches concerned should agree among themselves on each occasion which of them should appoint members of the Committee. It may be that when the Assembly meets it will modify this procedure. Such difficulties as exist arise from the need to keep the size of the Committee within the limits appropriate to committee work and to comparatively frequent meetings.

6. *Commissions*: These form a familiar part of the machinery of the Life and Work and the Faith and Order movements. It will be noticed that the Faith and Order Commission is to be conducted on the basis hitherto accepted by that movement. Members of commissions need not be members of the Assembly or Central Committee, and may include persons who are members of churches which have not joined the Council. Thus it is hoped that the establishment of the World Council will not involve any narrowing of the area of cooperation hitherto enjoyed in this field.

7. *Other ecumenical Christian organizations*: A world council of churches should be in touch with the confessional world organizations of the churches and with the main Christian activities which are organized on a worldwide scale — such as the great youth organizations, the World Alliance for International Friendship through the Churches, and, not in the last place, the International Missionary Council.

8. *Amendments*: Evidently provision must be made for amendments to the constitution. But in the case of an organization to which the churches have given their consent, special safeguards are needed. The clause aims at providing adequate safeguards without rendering the difficulties of amendment insuperable.

III. Ad-interim administration

The conference at Utrecht invited the members of the Committee of Fourteen and their alternates appointed by the Oxford and Edinburgh conferences, to serve as a Provisional Committee, together with such additional members, not exceeding three in each instance, as the Administrative Committee of Life and Work and the Continuation Committee of the Edinburgh conference might appoint, should they desire to do so. This Committee will exercise only such powers and functions as may be approved by the Administrative Committee of Life and Work or the Continuation Committee of Faith and Order.

It is understood that all arrangements and appointments made by the Provisional Committee are provisional, and that the World Council is entirely free to determine the tasks which it will undertake and the provision in personnel and finance required for carrying them out.

The conference requested the Provisional Committee to make such arrangements and appointments as may be required for the maintenance of the work of the Life and Work and the Faith and Order movements. The conference suggested that the Provisional Committee should appoint a small administrative committee to act on its behalf until its next meeting. The appointment of the Provisional Committee was officially confirmed by action of the Life and Work Administrative Committee in May 1938 and of the Faith and Order Continuation Committee in August 1938.

Statement on "The Church, the churches and the World Council of Churches"

The ecclesiological significance of the World Council of Churches*

I. Introduction

The first Assembly at Amsterdam adopted a resolution on "the authority of the Council" which read:

> The World Council of Churches is composed of churches which acknowledge Jesus Christ as God and Saviour. They find their unity in him. They do not have to create their unity; it is the gift of God. But they know that it is their duty to make common cause in the search for the expression of that unity in work and in life. The Council desires to serve the churches which are its constituent members as an instrument whereby they may bear witness together to their common allegiance to Jesus Christ, and cooperate in matters requiring united action. But the Council is far from desiring to usurp any of the functions which already belong to its constituent churches, or to control them, or to legislate for them, and indeed is prevented by its constitution from doing so. Moreover, while earnestly seeking fellowship in thought and action for all its members, the Council disavows any thought of becoming a single unified church structure independent of the churches which have joined in constituting the Council, or a structure dominated by a centralized administrative authority.
>
> The purpose of the Council is to express its unity in another way. Unity arises out of the love of God in Jesus Christ, which, binding the constituent churches to him, binds them to one another. It is the earnest desire of the Council that the churches may be bound closer to Christ and therefore closer to one another. In the bond of his love, they will desire

---

*This statement was received by the Central Committee of the World Council of Churches, Toronto, 1950, and commended for study and comment in the churches.

continually to pray for one another and to strengthen one another, in worship and in witness, bearing one another's burdens and so fulfilling the law of Christ.

This statement authoritatively answered some of the questions which had arisen about the nature of the Council. But it is clear that other questions are now arising and some attempt to answer them must be made, especially in the face of a number of false or inadequate conceptions of the Council which are being presented.

II. The need for further statement

The World Council of Churches represents a new and unprecedented approach to the problem of interchurch relationships. Its purpose and nature can be easily misunderstood. So it is salutary that we should state more clearly and definitely what the World Council is and what it is not.

This more precise definition involves certain difficulties. It is not for nothing that the churches themselves have refrained from giving detailed and precise definitions of the nature of the Church. If this is true of them, it is not to be expected that the World Council can easily achieve a definition which has to take account of all the various ecclesiologies of its member churches. The World Council deals in a provisional way with divisions between existing churches, which ought not to be, because they contradict the very nature of the Church. A situation such as this cannot be met in terms of well-established precedents. The main problem is how one can formulate the ecclesiological implications of a body in which so many different conceptions of the Church are represented, without using the categories or language of one particular conception of the Church.

In order to clarify the notion of the World Council of Churches it will be best to begin by a series of negations so as to do away at the outset with certain misunderstandings which may easily arise or have already arisen, because of the newness and unprecedented character of the underlying conception.

III. What the World Council of Churches is not

1. *The World Council of Churches is not and must never become a superchurch.*

It is not a superchurch. It is not the world church. It is not the Una Sancta of which the Creeds speak. This misunderstanding arises again and again although it has been denied as clearly as possible in official pronouncements of the Council. It is based on complete ignorance of the real situation within the Council. For if the Council should in any way violate its own constitutional principle, that it cannot legislate or act for its member churches, it would cease to maintain the support of its membership.

In speaking of "member churches", we repeat a phrase from the Constitution of the World Council of Churches; but membership in the Council does not in any sense mean that the churches belong to a body which can take decisions for them. Each church retains the constitutional right to ratify or to reject utterances or actions of the Council. The "authority" of the Council consists only "in the weight which it carries with the churches by its own wisdom" (William Temple).

2. *The purpose of the World Council of Churches is not to negotiate unions between churches, which can only be done by the churches themselves acting on their own initiative, but to bring the churches into living contact with each other and to promote the study and discussion of the issues of Church unity.*

By its very existence and its activities the Council bears witness to the necessity of a clear manifestation of the oneness of the Church of Christ. But it remains the right and duty of each church to draw from its ecumenical experience such consequences as it feels bound to do on the basis of its own convictions. No church, therefore, need fear that the Council will press it into decisions concerning union with other churches.

3. *The World Council cannot and should not be based on any one particular conception of the Church. It does not prejudge the ecclesiological problem.*

It is often suggested that the dominating or underlying conception of the Council is that of such a church or such and such a school of theology. It may well be that at a certain particular conference or in a particular utterance one can find traces of the strong influence of a certain tradition or theology.

The Council as such cannot possibly become the instrument of one confession or school without losing its very *raison d'être*. There is room and space in the World Council for the ecclesiology of every church which is ready to participate in the ecumenical conversation and which takes its stand on the Basis of the Council, which is "a fellowship of churches which accept our Lord Jesus Christ as God and Saviour''.

4. *Membership in the World Council of Churches does not imply that a church treats its own conception of the Church as merely relative.*

There are critics, and not infrequently friends, of the ecumenical movement who criticize or praise it for its alleged inherent latitudinarianism. According to them the ecumenical movement stands for the fundamental equality of all Christian doctrines and conceptions of the Church and is, therefore, not concerned with the question of truth. This misunderstanding is due to the fact that ecumenism has in the minds of these persons become identified with certain particular theories about unity, which have indeed played a role in ecumenical history, but which do not represent the common view of the movement as a whole, and have never been officially endorsed by the World Council.

5. *Membership in the World Council does not imply the acceptance of a specific doctrine concerning the nature of Church unity.*

The Council stands for Church unity. But in its midst there are those who conceive unity wholly or largely as a full consensus in the realm of doctrine, others who conceive of it primarily as sacramental communion based on common church order, others who consider both indispensable, others who would only require unity in certain fundamentals of faith and order, again others who conceive the one Church exclusively as a universal spiritual fellowship, or hold that visible unity is inessential or even undesirable. But none of these conceptions can be called the ecumenical theory. The whole point of the ecumenical conversation is precisely that all these conceptions enter into dynamic relations with each other.

In particular, membership in the World Council does not imply acceptance or rejection of the doctrine that the unity of the Church consists in the unity of the invisible Church. Thus the statement in the Encyclical *Mystici Corporis* concerning what it considers the error of a spiritualized conception of unity does not apply to the World Council. The World Council does not ''imagine a church which one cannot see or touch, which would be only spiritual, in which numerous Christian bodies, though divided in matters of faith, would nevertheless be united through an invisible link''. It does,

however, include churches which believe that the Church is essentially invisible as well as those which hold that visible unity is essential.

IV. The assumptions underlying the World Council of Churches

We must now try to define the positive assumptions which underlie
the World Council of Churches and the ecclesiological implications
of membership in it.

1. *The member churches of the Council believe that conversation,
cooperation and common witness of the churches must be based on
the common recognition that Christ is the Divine Head of the Body.*

The Basis of the World Council is the acknowledgment of the central fact that "other foundation can no man lay than that is laid,
even Jesus Christ". It is the expression of the conviction that the
Lord of the Church is God-among-us who continues to gather his
children and to build his Church himself.

Therefore, no relationship between the churches can have any
substance or promise unless it starts with the common submission of
the churches to the headship of Jesus Christ in his Church. From different points of view churches ask: "How can men with opposite
convictions belong to one and the same federation of the faithful?"
A clear answer to that question was given by the Orthodox delegates
in Edinburgh 1937 when they said: "In spite of all our differences,
our common Master and Lord is *one* — Jesus Christ who will lead us
to a more and more close collaboration for the edifying of the Body
of Christ." The fact of Christ's headship over his people compels all
those who acknowledge him to enter into real and close relationships
with each other — even though they differ in many important points.

2. *The member churches of the World Council believe on the basis
of the New Testament that the Church of Christ is one.*

The ecumenical movement owes its existence to the fact that this
article of the faith has again come home to men and women in many
churches with an inescapable force. As they face the discrepancy between the truth that there is and can only be one Church of Christ,
and the fact that there exist so many churches which claim to be churches of Christ but are not in living unity with each other, they feel a
holy dissatisfaction with the present situation. The churches realize
that it is a matter of simple Christian duty for each church to do its
utmost for the manifestation of the Church in its oneness, and to

work and pray that Christ's purpose for his Church should be fulfilled.

3. *The member churches recognize that the membership of the Church of Christ is more inclusive than the membership of their own church body. They seek, therefore, to enter into living contact with those outside their own ranks who confess the Lordship of Christ.*

All the Christian churches, including the Church of Rome, hold that there is no complete identity between the membership of the Church Universal and the membership of their own church. They recognize that there are church members "extra muros", that these belong "aliquo modo" to the Church, or even that there is an "ecclesia extra ecclesiam". This recognition finds expression in the fact that with very few exceptions the Christian churches accept the baptism administered by other churches as valid.

But the question arises what consequences are to be drawn from this teaching. Most often in church history the churches have only drawn the negative consequence that they should have no dealings with those outside their membership. The underlying assumption of the ecumenical movement is that each church has a positive task to fulfill in this realm. That task is to seek fellowship with all those who, while not members of the same visible body, belong together as members of the mystical body. And the ecumenical movement is the place where this search and discovery take place.

4. *The member churches of the World Council consider the relationship of other churches to the Holy Catholic Church which the Creeds profess as a subject for mutual consideration. Nevertheless, membership does not imply that each church must regard the other member churches as churches in the true and full sense of the word.*

There is a place in the World Council both for those churches which recognize other churches as churches in the full and true sense, and for those which do not. But these divided churches, even if they cannot yet accept each other as true and pure churches, believe that they should not remain in isolation from each other, and consequently they have associated themselves in the World Council of Churches.

They know that differences of faith and order exist, but they recognize one another as serving the one Lord, and they wish to explore their differences in mutual respect, trusting that they may thus be led by the Holy Spirit to manifest their unity in Christ.

5. *The member churches of the World Council recognize in other churches elements of the true Church. They consider that this mutual recognition obliges them to enter into a serious conversation with each other in the hope that these elements of truth will lead to the recognition of the full truth and to unity based on the full truth.*

It is generally taught in the different churches that other churches have certain elements of the true Church, in some traditions called "vestigia ecclesiae". Such elements are the preaching of the Word, the teaching of the Holy Scriptures and the administration of the sacraments. These elements are more than pale shadows of the life of the true Church. They are a fact of real promise and provide an opportunity to strive by frank and brotherly intercourse for the realization of a fuller unity. Moreover, Christians of all ecclesiological views throughout the world, by the preaching of the Gospel, brought men and women to salvation by Christ, to newness of life in him, and into Christian fellowship with one another.

The ecumenical movement is based upon the conviction that these "traces" are to be followed. The churches should not despise them as mere elements of truth but rejoice in them as hopeful signs pointing towards real unity. For what are these elements? Not dead remnants of the past but powerful means by which God works. Questions may and must be raised about the validity and purity of teaching and sacramental life, but there can be no question that such dynamic elements of church life justify the hope that the churches which maintain them will be led into full truth. It is through the ecumenical conversation that this recognition of truth is facilitated.

6. *The member churches of the Council are willing to consult together in seeking to learn of the Lord Jesus Christ what witness he would have them to bear to the world in his name.*

Since the very *raison d'être* of the Church is to witness to Christ, churches cannot meet together without seeking from their common Lord a common witness before the world. This will not always be possible. But when it proves possible thus to speak or act together, the churches can gratefully accept it as God's gracious gift that in spite of their disunity he has enabled them to render one and the same witness and that they may thus manifest something of the unity, the purpose of which is precisely "that the world may believe", and that they may "testify that the Father has sent the Son to be the Saviour of the world".

7. *A further practical implication of common membership in the World Council is that the member churches should recognize their solidarity with each other, render assistance to each other in case of need, and refrain from such actions as are incompatible with brotherly relationship.*

Within the Council the churches seek to deal with each other with a brotherly concern. This does not exclude extremely frank speaking to each other, in which within the Council the churches ask each other searching questions and face their differences. But this is to be done for the building up of the Body of Christ. This excludes a purely negative attitude of one church to another. The positive affirmation of each church's faith is to be welcomed, but actions incompatible with brotherly relationship towards other member churches defeat the very purpose for which the Council has been created. On the contrary, these churches should help each other in removing all obstacles to the free exercise of the Church's normal functions. And whenever a church is in need or under persecution, it should be able to count on the help of the other churches through the Council.

8. *The member churches enter into spiritual relationships through which they seek to learn from each other and to give help to each other in order that the Body of Christ may be built up and that the life of the churches may be renewed.*

It is the common teaching of the churches that the Church as the temple of God is at the same time a building which has been built and a building which is being built. The Church has, therefore, aspects which belong to its very structure and essence and cannot be changed. But it has other aspects which are subject to change. Thus the life of the Church, as it expresses itself in its witness to its own members and to the world, needs constant renewal. The churches can and should help each other in this realm by a mutual exchange of thought and of experience. This is the significance of the study work of the World Council and of many other of its activities. There is no intention to impose any particular pattern of thought or life upon the churches. But whatever insight has been received by one or more churches is to be made available to all the churches for the sake of the "building up of the Body of Christ".

None of these positive assumptions, implied in the existence of the World Council, is in conflict whith the teachings of the member churches. We believe therefore that no church need fear that by entering into the World Council it is in danger of denying its heritage.

As the conversation between the churches develops and as the churches enter into closer contact with each other, they will no doubt have to face new decisions and problems. For the Council exists to break the deadlock between the churches. But in no case can or will any church be pressed to take a decision against its own conviction or desire. The churches remain wholly free in the action which, on the basis of their convictions and in the light of their ecumenical contacts, they will or will not take.

A very real unity has been discovered in ecumenical meetings which is, to all who collaborate in the World Council, the most precious element of its life. It exists and we receive it again and again as an unmerited gift from the Lord. We praise God for this foretaste of the unity of his people and continue hopefully with the work to which he has called us together. For the Council exists to serve the churches as they prepare to meet their Lord who knows only one flock.

Notes

Preface

1. Archbishop Germanos, *The Ecumenical Review*, Vol. I, No. 1, 1948. Prof. Istavrides, *The Ecumenical Review*, Vol. XI, 1958-1959. S. McCrea Cavert, *The American Churches in the Ecumenical Movement 1900-1968*, New York, Association Press, 1968.

2. N. Karlström, "Ein ökumenischer Kirchenrat", *Ökumenische Einheit*, Vol. III, No. 2, 1953. F. Iremonger, *Archbishop William Temple: His Life and Letters*, London, Oxford University Press, 1948. R. Jasper, *George Bell, Bishop of Chichester*, London, Oxford University Press, 1967. Marc Boegner, *The Long Road Towards Unity*, London, Collins, 1970. Schmidt, *Architect of Unity: a Biography of S. McCrea Cavert*, New York, Friendship Press, 1978. Bengt Sundkler, *Nathan Söderblom: His Life and Work*, Lund, Gleerups, 1968.

3. Charles MacFarland, *Steps Toward the World Council*, New York, Fleming Revell, 1938. William Adams Brown, *Towards a United Church*, New York, Scribners, 1946.

4. Ruth Rouse and Stephen Neill (eds.), London, SPCK, 1954. See also chapter 12 of my *Memoirs*, London, SCM, and Philadelphia, Westminster, 1973.

5. Paris, Desclée de Brouwer, 1962.

6. Paris, Beauchesne, 1972.

7. Several were described in *The Ecumenical Review*, Vol. I, No. 1, 1948.

Chapter 1

1. *The Ecumenical Review*, Vol. XI, 1958-1959, p. 292.

2. See the report of the delegation in Faith and Order pamphlet No. 32B, p. 29.

3. See Appendix I. The translation given in the appendix is a corrected translation, printed in *The Ecumenical Review*, Vol. XII, 1959, p. 79.

4. Nathan Söderblom, *Pater Pribilla und die ökumenische Erweckung*, Uppsala, Almqvist & Wiksells, 1931, p. 6.

5. Report, p. 30.

6. Ephesians 3:6.

7. *Die Eiche*, 1929, p. 30.

8. *The Ecumenical Review*, 1948, Vol. 1, No. 1, p. 88.

9. The Orthodox Church of Russia could not be represented. But church leaders from the Russian emigration were present.

10. *The Ecumenical Review*, 1948, Vol. 1, No. 1, p. 88.

11. Faith and Order pamphlet No. 34, "A Compilation of Proposals for Christian Unity", pp. 78-79.

12. Nikolaus Glubokovski *et al.*, *Den orthodoxa Kristenheten och Kirkens Enhet*, Stockholm, Svenska Kyrkans Diakonistyrelses Bokförlag, 1921, p. 169.

13. *The Christian Union Quarterly*, Vol. XVII, p. 242.

Chapter 3

1. Nils Karlström, "Ein ökumenischer Kirchenrat", *Ökumenische Einheit*, 1952, II, 100.

2. *Kristna Samförstandsträvander, under Världskriget 1914-1918*, Stockholm, Svenska Kyrkans Diakonistyrelses Bokförlag, 1947, p. 458.

3. *Christian Fellowship*, New York, Fleming Revell, 1923, p. 188. And *Die Einigung der Christenheit*, Halle, Müllers Verlag, 1925.

4. *The Contemporary Review*, 1919, Vol. 116, pp. 309-315. *Die Eiche*, 1919, pp. 124-136. Extracts are given in Appendix II.

5. Bengt Sundkler, *Nathan Söderblom: His Life and Work*, Lund, Gleerups, 1968, p. 230.

6. *The Ecumenical Review*, Vol. I, No. 1, 1948, p. 88.

Chapter 4

1. New York, Fleming Revell, 1923, pp. 208-209.

2. George Bell, *The Stockholm Conference 1925: Official Report*, London, Oxford University Press, 1926, p. 706.

3. *Steps Toward the World Council*, New York, Fleming Revell, 1938, p. 93.

4. German official report, p. 684, in the author's translation, which brings out the main point more clearly than the translation in the English official report, p. 691.

5. *Op. cit*, p. 51. See also p. 69.

6. *Op. cit.* (English report), pp. 682-683.

7. Bengt Sundkler, *Nathan Söderblom: His Life and Work*, Lund, Gleerups, 1968, pp. 379-380.

Chapter 5
1. *Faith and Order: Lausanne 1927*, London, SCM, 1927, p. 397.
2. William Adams Brown, *Towards a United Church*, New York, Scribners, 1946, p. 108.
3. "To act together, as if the churches were one body" could be taken to mean: to assume a role which did not express the real situation. The Roman Catholic theologians, Charles Journet (*L'union des Eglises*, Paris, Grasset, 1927, pp. 83-84) and Yves Congar (*Divided Christendom*, London, Bles, 1939, p. 118) criticized Life and Work sharply for using the "as if" principle and thus embracing theological relativism.

Chapter 6
1. Bengt Sundkler, *Nathan Söderblom: His Life and Work*, Lund, Gleerups, 1968, p. 414.
2. Nathan Söderblom, *Pater Pribilla und die ökumenische Erweckung*, Uppsala, Almqvist & Wiksells, 1931.

Chapter 7
1. *Die Eiche*, 1932, No. 4, p. 311. See also p. 308, p. 318 and p. 334.

Chapter 8
1. *Die Eiche*, 1932, No. 4, p. 334: address to the Ecumenical Youth Conference in Czechoslovakia.
2. Letter to John R. Mott of 14 November 1934. See William R. Hogg, *Ecumenical Foundations*, New York, Harper, 1952, pp. 284 and 421.
3. *Minutes*, meeting, Life and Work, Fanö 1934, p. 48.
4. "Reflections on Edinburgh 1910", *Religion and Life*, summer 1960.
5. Oldham at the Life and Work meeting at Chamby 1935.

Chapter 10
1. "Next Steps on the Road to a United Church", 1937, p. 41.
2. *Ibid.*, p. 43.

Chapter 11
1. S. McCrea Cavert, *On the Road to Christian Unity*, New York, Harper, 1961, p. 24.
2. See Appendix III.
3. World Alliance, *News Letter*, April 1950.

Chapter 12
1. Leonard Hodgson, ed., *The Second World Conference on Faith and Order*, Edinburgh 1937, London, SCM, 1938, pp. 194-196.
2. *Ibid.*, p. 340.

3. *Ibid.*, p. 151.

4. William Adams Brown, *Towards a United Church*, New York, Scribners, 1946, p. 141.

5. *The Second World Conference on Faith and Order*, p. 368.

6. *Ibid.*, p. 268-269.

7. Fourth Survey of the Affairs of the Continental Churches.

8. Münich, Kaiser Verlag, 1973, p. 242.

9. Hodgson, *op. cit.*, p. 185.

10. *Op. cit.*, p. 152.

Chapter 13

1. *The World Council of Churches: Its Process of Formation*, minutes and reports of the meeting of the Provisional Committee of the WCC held in Geneva, 1946, p. 175.

2. *Op. cit.*, p. 182.

Chapter 14

1. Armin Boyens, *Kirchenkampf und Ökumene 1939-1945*, Münich, Kaiser Verlag, 1973, p. 246.

Chapter 15

1. See Appendix IV.

2. *The World Council of Churches: Its Process of Formation*, minutes and reports of the meeting of the Provisional Committee of the WCC, Geneva, 1946, p. 172-173.

Chapter 17

1. *The World Council of Churches: Its Process of Formation*, minutes and reports of the meeting of the Provisional Committee of the WCC held in Geneva, 1946, p. 75.

2. *Ibid.*, p. 14.

Chapter 19

1. See my *Memoirs*, pp. 205-208.

2. *The First Assembly of the World Council of Churches*, Amsterdam 1948, London, SCM Press, 1949, p. 217.

3. *Ibid.*, p. 216.

4. *Ibid.*, p. 214.

5. *Ibid.*, p. 28.

6. *Ibid.*, pp. 127-128.

Chapter 20

1. *Christendom*, summer 1946 and autumn 1946.

2. "Le Conseil oecuménique des Eglises: sa nature, ses limites", *Hommage et reconnaissance, 60 ans de Karl Barth*, Neuchâtel, Delachaux et Niestlé, 1946.

3. *The Universal Church in God's Design*, London, SCM Press, 1948, p. 196.

4. *Ibid.*, p. 195.

5. The RC participants were: R.P. Congar OP, R.P. Danielou SJ, Abbé Desmettre, R.P. Dumont OP, M. Jean Guitton, R.P. Hamer OP, R.P. Lialine CSB, Abbé Michalon, R.P. Rouquette SJ and R.P. Villain SM.

6. See Appendix V.

7. *Report of the Third World Conference on Faith and Order, Lund*, London, SCM, 1953, p. 135.

8. *The Christian Hope and the Task of the Church: Six Ecumenical Surveys*, New York, Harper, 1954, p. 9.

9. See *The Ecumenical Review*, Vol. VIII, No. 1, October 1955.

10. The importance of the discussion concerning the Basis for the self-understanding of the Council is shown in the remarkable book of Wolfdieter Theurer, *Die Trinitarische Basis des Ökumenischen Rates*, Frankfurt, Gerhard Kaffke, 1967.

11. *The New Delhi Report*, Third Assembly of the WCC, London, SCM, 1962, p. 117.

12. *The Fourth World Conference on Faith and Order*, Montreal 1963, London, SCM, 1964, p. 49.

13. *La signification écclésiologique du Conseil oecuménique des Eglises, 1945-1963*, Lyon, Facultés catholiques, 1972, p. 107.

14. *Minutes*, Central Committee Toronto 1950, p. 14.

15. *Conflict over the Ecumenical Movement*, Geneva, WCC, 1981, p. 311.

16. *Ibid.*, pp. 314-315.

Chapter 21

1. Nathan Söderblom, *Pater Max Pribilla und die ökumenische Erweckung*, Uppsala, Almqvist Wiksells, 1931, pp. 40-41.

2. Quoted by N. Ehrenström, in *A History of the Ecumenical Movement, 1947-1948*, eds Ruth Rouse and Stephen Neill, London, SPCK, 1954, p. 571.

3. *The First Assembly of the World Council of Churches*, Amsterdam 1948, London, SCM Press, 1949, p. 29.

4. Bengt Sundkler, *Nathan Söderblom: His Life and Work*, Lund, Gleerups, 1968, p. 230.

5. Leonard Hodgson, *The Second World Conference on Faith and Order*, Edinburgh 1937, London, SCM Press, 1938, p. 196.

6. *The First Assembly of the WCC*, p. 127.

7. Charles S. MacFarland, *Steps Toward the World Council*, New York, Fleming Revell, 1938, p. 104.

8. *Op. cit.*, p. 108.

Index of names